Harmony in Conflict

Finding Common Ground with Challenging Personalities

Marcus Lee

Table of Contents

INTRODUCTION

We come across a diverse range of personalities in the tapestry of our lives, which is woven together by the strands of innumerable relationships. Some simply become notes in the symphony of our lives, while others are discordant, testing our tolerance, compassion, and comprehension. These difficult individuals have the power to upend our peace and leave us perplexed, angry, or even hurt. However, these very people present us with chances for development, change, and the meaningful finding of shared ground.

Welcome to "Harmony in Conflict: Finding Common Ground with Challenging Personalities." This book takes us on a deep dive into the complex dynamics of human interaction through a voyage of exploration and discovery. We will make our way through the maze of personalities, unraveling the puzzles of why certain people are so hard to relate to, and others are so easy.

It's not just a skill to comprehend, relate to, and find common ground with difficult personalities; it's an art form that enables us to turn discord into harmony, conflict into cooperation, and frustration into fulfillment. With the help of psychological, communication, and real-world experiences, we will provide you with a newfound perspective, valuable tools, and techniques to help you successfully negotiate the complex waters of interpersonal relationships.

We invite you to be open to the possibilities that lie ahead as we set out on this life-changing journey. Together, we will discover the keys to establishing enduring harmony with even the most difficult personalities, creating connections beyond disagreement and resulting in more satisfying, richer relationships.

CHAPTER I

Understanding Personality Types

Introduction to different personality types

The range of human behaviors, thoughts, and emotional reactions is astounding. The complexities of our distinct personality types contribute to this diversity. Not only are these personality types fascinating, but they are also crucial for developing stronger interpersonal bonds, more transparent communication, and personal development. We will examine several models and frameworks that provide insights into what makes each of us unique as we delve into the introduction of various personality types in this section.

The Myers-Briggs Type Indicator (MBTI) is a well-known framework for comprehending personality types. The MBTI, created by Katharine Cook Briggs and her daughter Isabel Briggs Myers, divides people into 16 personality types according to four dichotomies: extraversion versus introversion, sensing versus intuition, thinking versus feeling, and perceiving versus judging. When these four preferences are combined, a comprehensive personality profile of the individual is produced. For instance, an INFP (Introverted, Intuitive, Feeling, Perceiving) person is typically flexible in their outlook on life, intuitive, introverted, and driven by their emotions. The MBTI offers insightful information about how individuals think, act, and relate to others.

The Big Five Personality Traits, sometimes called the Five Factor Model, is another popular model. Openness to Experience, Conscientiousness, Extraversion,

Agreeableness, and Neuroticism are the five broad dimensions into which this model divides personality (often abbreviated as OCEAN). People fall somewhere along the spectrums represented by each of these dimensions. Someone with a high extraversion level, for example, is gregarious, extroverted, and finds social situations stimulating, whereas someone with a low extraversion level might prefer solitude and find social situations taxing. The Big Five model looks at essential characteristics that affect responses and behavior to give a more complex understanding of personality.

Another well-liked personality system is the Enneagram, which examines nine fundamental personality types, each with distinct tendencies, fears, and motivations. The Enneagram explores people's underlying motivations and desires in addition to their outward behaviors. For instance, a Type Two, also referred to as "The Helper," is driven by the need to be needed and loved, which can result in selflessness and a propensity to put the needs of others before their own. A Type Five, or "The Investigator," on the other hand, is more interested in knowledge and comprehension, which frequently leads to reflection and a search for subject-matter expertise. The Enneagram facilitates personal development and improved interpersonal relationships by assisting people in becoming more self-aware and understanding of their underlying motivations.

While these models offer insightful information, it's crucial to remember that they do not fully capture the intricacies of the human psyche. There are also other systems and cultural differences to consider. For example, the DISC assessment categorizes people into four primary personality types: dominance, influence, steadiness, and conscientiousness. These methods are often employed in professional settings to enhance communication and teamwork. In some cultures, astrology and zodiac signs are utilized to predict personality traits and compatibility.

It's essential to recognize that personality is not a static attribute but a dynamic and ever-evolving aspect of the individual, independent of these models and frameworks. A person's personality can evolve over time due to a variety of factors, including age, life experiences, and personal development. Furthermore, people are multifaceted and can exhibit a range of traits and behaviors depending on the situation; they are not confined to a single personality type or trait.

Understanding diverse personality types has practical implications that can significantly impact various aspects of one's life. By respecting and acknowledging personality differences, we can foster more harmonious interactions and reduce conflict in personal relationships. In the workplace, recognizing the personality types of coworkers can enhance collaboration and teamwork. Self-awareness of one's own personality type can aid in goal-setting and personal growth. Essentially, the study of personality types is a valuable tool for navigating the intricate web of interpersonal relationships and forging closer bonds with others.

In conclusion, learning about the various personality types is an intriguing exploration of the complex nature of people. Psychometric models such as the MBTI, Big Five Personality Traits, and Enneagram provide essential insights into people's worldviews, decision-making processes, and interpersonal relationships. Although these frameworks offer a basis for understanding personality, it is crucial to remember that personality is dynamic and subject to the influence of numerous factors. Accepting the variety of personality types can improve relationships, communication, and personal development, all of which contribute to enriching our experiences in the complex web of human connection.

Myers-Briggs Type Indicator (MBTI)

The Myers-Briggs Type Indicator (or MBTI) is a widely recognized and extensively used personality assessment tool that has fascinated individuals, organizations, and psychologists for decades. Developed by Katharine Cook Briggs along with her daughter Isabel Briggs Myers in the early to mid-20th century, the MBTI aims to give individuals a deeper understanding of their personalities and how they relate to the world. This section explores the MBTI's history, structure, and implications, shedding light on its enduring popularity and its role in personal and professional development.

At the core of the MBTI lies the belief that there are fundamental differences in how individuals perceive and interact with the world. This framework is based on Carl Jung's theory of psychological types, which suggests that people exhibit consistent behavior patterns, thinking, and feeling. Jung's ideas were the foundation upon which Katharine Cook Briggs and Isabel Briggs Myers built the MBTI. Their goal was to create a practical tool to help people better understand themselves and others, ultimately facilitating improved communication and collaboration.

According to the MBTI, people can be categorized as 1 of 16 personality types depending on how they combine the four dichotomies of extraversion versus introversion, sensing versus intuition, thinking versus feeling, and perceiving versus judging. Each person is assigned one preference from each pair of these dichotomies, which stand for opposing preferences, based on how they answer a series of questions. For instance, someone who prefers extraversion is more likely to be sociable, energized by social interactions, and focused on the external world, while an introvert tends to be more reserved, introspective, and oriented toward the inner world of thoughts and ideas.

The MBTI divides these four preferences into dichotomies and combines them to create the 16 personality types, each represented by a four-letter code. For example, an INFP personality type signifies Introverted, Intuitive, Feeling, and Perceiving preferences. These codes serve as a shorthand way to describe an individual's personality and provide a glimpse into their cognitive processes and decision-making tendencies.

One of the strengths of the MBTI is its simplicity and accessibility. The assessment can be administered relatively quickly, and the results are simple to understand and discuss. This accessibility has contributed to its widespread use in various settings, including workplaces, educational institutions, and personal development programs. Many people find it valuable to discover their MBTI type, as it can offer insights into their communication style, career preferences, and interpersonal relationships.

However, it's essential to acknowledge that the MBTI has also faced criticism and skepticism over the years. Some psychologists argue that it oversimplifies the complexities of human personality and that the four-letter codes may not fully capture the richness and variability of individual behavior. Additionally, the MBTI has been criticized for its lack of empirical support, as it does not always yield consistent results upon retesting.

Despite these criticisms, many individuals and organizations continue to embrace the MBTI. Its enduring popularity is partly attributed to its positive and affirming approach to personality assessment. Unlike some other assessments that focus on identifying weaknesses or pathologies, the MBTI emphasizes the inherent value of each personality type and encourages individuals to embrace their unique strengths and contributions.

In personal and professional development, the MBTI can be a valuable tool for fostering self-awareness and empathy. By having a knowledge with their own personality type and those of others, individuals can become more effective communicators, collaborators, and leaders. For example, a manager who recognizes that their team includes both introverted and extraverted individuals can tailor their leadership style to accommodate their team members' diverse needs and preferences, ultimately promoting a more harmonious and productive work environment.

In conclusion, the Myers-Briggs Type Indicator (MBTI) offers a structured framework for understanding human personality and behavior. While it has its critics and limitations, the MBTI continues to play a significant role in personal and professional development by providing individuals with valuable insights into their preferences and those around them. Its simplicity and accessibility make it a practical tool for fostering self-awareness, improving communication, and enhancing relationships. Ultimately, the enduring popularity of the MBTI highlights the enduring human fascination with understanding what makes us who we are and how we can navigate the complexities of human interaction.

The Big Five Personality Traits

The study of human personality has been a subject of fascination and inquiry for centuries. Among the numerous theories and models that attempt to explain the complexities of personality, the Big Five Personality Traits, or the Five Factor Model, stands as one of the most widely recognized and influential frameworks. This section aims to provide a comprehensive exploration of the Big Five Personality Traits, delving into their history, structure, practical applications, and enduring significance in the fields of psychology, personal development, and organizational behavior.

The Big Five Personality Traits, often abbreviated as OCEAN, represent five fundamental dimensions of human personality. These dimensions are Openness to Experience, Conscientiousness, Extraversion, Agreeableness, and Neuroticism. Each trait exists on a spectrum, and individuals fall somewhere along each spectrum, creating a unique personality profile. These traits are considered relatively stable throughout an individual's life and provide valuable insights into how people perceive the world, interact with others, and make decisions.

The first dimension, Openness to Experience, reflects an individual's receptivity to new ideas, experiences, and novelty. Those high in Openness tend to be imaginative, curious, and open-minded. They embrace change and are often drawn to artistic pursuits and intellectual exploration. In contrast, individuals low in Openness prefer routine, tradition, and familiarity, and they may be more conventional in their thinking and behavior.

Conscientiousness is the second dimension and pertains to an individual's level of organization, self-discipline, and goal-directedness. Highly conscientious individuals are diligent, detail-oriented, and reliable. They set and pursue ambitious goals and are often associated with high levels of achievement. On the other hand, those low in Conscientiousness may struggle with organization and may be more spontaneous and flexible in their approach to life.

Extraversion, the third dimension, represents an individual's degree of sociability, assertiveness, and comfort in social situations. Extraverts thrive on social interactions, are outgoing, and often seek the company of others to energize themselves. In contrast, introverts are more reserved and reflective and prefer solitude or smaller gatherings to recharge.

The fourth dimension, Agreeableness, reflects an individual's empathy, cooperativeness, and compassion level. Highly agreeable individuals are kind, considerate, and prioritize harmonious relationships. They are skilled at conflict resolution and tend to be trusting of others. Those low in Agreeableness may be more competitive, skeptical, and less inclined to prioritize the needs and feelings of others.

Neuroticism, the fifth and final dimension, relates to an individual's emotional stability and resilience in the face of stress and negative emotions. Highly neurotic individuals are prone to anxiety, worry, and mood swings. They may react strongly to stressors and find it challenging to bounce back from setbacks. Conversely, those low in Neuroticism tend to be emotionally stable, even-tempered, and better equipped to handle stress.

The origins of the Big Five Personality Traits can be traced back to the mid-20th century, but it wasn't until the 1980s and 1990s that researchers like Paul Costa and Robert McCrae further refined the model and popularized it in the field of psychology. Since then, the Big Five has gained widespread acceptance as a robust and comprehensive framework for understanding personality.

The practical applications of the Big Five Personality Traits are numerous and far-reaching. The model is used in psychology to study personality development, mental health, and interpersonal dynamics. Personality assessments based on the Big Five are commonly employed in clinical settings to aid in diagnosis and treatment planning. Additionally, the Big Five provides insights into how individuals might respond to various therapeutic interventions.

In the realm of personal development, the Big Five is a valuable tool for self-awareness and growth. Understanding one's own personality profile can inform career choices, relationship decisions, and personal goals.

For instance, a highly extraverted individual may find satisfaction in a career that involves frequent social interaction, while someone with high Conscientiousness may excel in roles that need meticulous attention to detail.

The Big Five also plays a significant role in organizational behavior and human resources. Many companies use personality assessments based on the Big Five to inform hiring decisions, team-building, and leadership development. For example, a manager may consider the personality traits of team members when forming project groups to ensure a balance of skills and characteristics that promote effective collaboration.

In conclusion, the Big Five Personality Traits represent a powerful and widely embraced framework for understanding human personality. Openness to Experience, Conscientiousness, Extraversion, Agreeableness, and Neuroticism offer valuable insights into the intricacies of how individuals think, feel, and behave. While the model has its critics and limitations, its enduring significance in psychology, personal development, and organizational behavior underscores its utility in helping individuals and organizations navigate the complexities of human interaction and personal growth. Whether used for self-discovery, therapy, or workplace dynamics, the Big Five Personality Traits continue to be a cornerstone in the study of human personality.

Enneagram Types

The Enneagram is a compelling and intricate personality system that has garnered significant attention in recent years, offering a unique perspective on the motivations and behaviors that drive individuals. Rooted in ancient spiritual traditions and further developed in modern psychology, the Enneagram categorizes individuals into nine distinct personality types, each characterized by specific traits, fears, desires, and core motivations. This section explores the Enneagram Types, delving into their origins, structure, practical applications, and the profound insights they offer into human nature.

The Enneagram's origins can be traced to various ancient traditions, including Sufism, Christianity, and Kabbalah. However, it was in the 20th century that it gained prominence and began to be integrated into psychological and self-development practices. Its modern evolution is often attributed to figures like Oscar Ichazo and Claudio Naranjo, who contributed to its development as a psychological tool.

The Enneagram system categorizes individuals into nine core personality types, each indicated by a number from one to nine. These types are interconnected on a complex diagram, known as the Enneagram symbol, which illustrates the relationships and dynamics among the types. Each personality type has unique characteristics, fears, desires, and motivations that drive their thoughts, emotions, and behaviors.

Type One, often called "The Perfectionist," is driven by a desire for perfection, integrity, and an aversion to mistakes. They are principled and often critical of themselves and others. Type Two, "The Helper," seeks love and approval through acts of service and assistance to others. They are nurturing and can be prone to people-pleasing tendencies. Type Three, "The Achiever," is motivated by success, recognition, and the desire to appear competent. They are often driven and goal-oriented.

Type Four, "The Individualist," desires uniqueness and authenticity. They are highly creative and sensitive but may struggle with feelings of inadequacy or being misunderstood. Type Five, "The Investigator," values knowledge and self-sufficiency. They are often reserved and seek understanding through in-depth analysis. Type Six, "The Loyalist," craves security and support. They are loyal and can be anxious or skeptical.

Type Seven, "The Enthusiast," seeks adventure, excitement, and avoidance of pain or discomfort. They are optimistic and tend to be spontaneous. Type Eight, "The Challenger," desires control and autonomy. They are assertive and may have a fear of being vulnerable or controlled. Type Nine, "The Peacemaker," values peace, harmony, and conflict avoidance. They are easygoing and may struggle with inertia or complacency.

What sets the Enneagram apart from other personality systems is its emphasis on core motivations and fears. While other systems often focus on observable behaviors, the Enneagram delves into the underlying drivers of those behaviors. For instance, a Type Two may engage in acts of service not just because it's a behavior they've adopted but because they fear rejection and believe that helping others will earn love and acceptance.

The Enneagram also acknowledges that individuals are not confined to a single personality type. Each type has a spectrum of healthy, average, and unhealthy traits, and individuals may move along this spectrum based on their life circumstances, personal growth, and stress levels. This fluidity adds depth to the Enneagram and allows for a more subtle understanding of personality.

Practically, the Enneagram can be used for personal development and growth. By identifying one's core Enneagram type, individuals gain insights into their patterns of strengths, behavior, and areas of potential growth. The system offers guidance on how to navigate challenges and cultivate healthier behaviors.

Additionally, the Enneagram is employed in therapeutic settings to aid in self-awareness and personal transformation. Therapists and counselors often use it to help clients explore their motivations, fears, and defenses, providing a more profound understanding of their emotional and psychological landscape.

In interpersonal relationships, the Enneagram can foster empathy and compassion. Understanding the Enneagram types of loved ones, friends, or colleagues can provide insight into their behaviors and reactions, promoting healthier communication and conflict resolution.

The Enneagram is used in the workplace for team-building, leadership development, and conflict resolution. By recognizing the Enneagram types of team members, managers can tailor their leadership approach to accommodate diverse personalities and strengths within the team.

In conclusion, the Enneagram Types offer a profound and multifaceted framework for understanding human motivations and behaviors. Rooted in ancient traditions and further developed in modern psychology, the Enneagram provides a unique perspective on personality that delves into core fears, desires, and motivations. Its practical applications in personal development, therapy, and interpersonal relationships make it a useful tool for self-discovery and growth. As individuals and organizations continue to seek more profound insights into human nature, the Enneagram stands as a powerful and evolving resource for unraveling the intricacies of the human psyche.

Strengths and weaknesses of personality typing systems

Personality typing systems are valuable tools for understanding and categorizing human behavior and characteristics. These systems offer insights into individual differences, help with self-awareness, and enhance interpersonal relationships. However, like any model or framework, they have their strengths and weaknesses. In this section, we will explore the advantages and limitations of personality typing systems, shedding light on the complexities of human personality assessment.

One of the primary strengths of personality typing systems is their ability to provide structure and organization to the vast diversity of human behavior. These systems categorize individuals into distinct types or categories, making it easier to describe and understand their personality traits, tendencies, and preferences. This structure can be beneficial for individuals seeking self-awareness and personal growth. By identifying their personality type, individuals can gain insight into their strengths as well as weaknesses, allowing them to make educated decisions and navigate their lives more effectively.

Moreover, personality typing systems often offer practical and actionable insights. For example, the Myers-Briggs Type Indicator (MBTI) provides specific guidance on communication styles, decision-making processes, and potential career paths based on an individual's type. This practical advice can be valuable for personal development, career planning, and relationship improvement.

Another strength of personality typing systems is their contribution to improved communication and understanding among individuals. People with a common framework for discussing personality differences are better equipped to empathize with others and adjust their communication styles accordingly. This can result in more harmonious relationships, reduced conflict, and enhanced teamwork in personal and professional contexts.

However, personality typing systems are not without their weaknesses and limitations. One of the most significant drawbacks is the potential for oversimplification. Human personality is complex and multifaceted, and attempting to categorize it into a limited number of types or traits can lead to a reductionist view of individuals. Critics argue that this oversimplification can ignore the nuances and unique qualities that make each person an individual.

Furthermore, personality typing systems may lack empirical validation. While some systems, like the Big Five Personality Traits, have a substantial body of research supporting their validity and reliability, others may lack scientific rigor. This raises concerns about the accuracy and legitimacy of specific typing systems. For instance, some critics argue that astrological personality typing systems lack scientific credibility.

Another limitation of personality typing systems is the potential for individuals to be confined by their type. People may identify so strongly with their assigned type that they limit themselves and their potential. This phenomenon is known as the "typecast effect," where individuals may believe they are bound by the characteristics associated with their type and fail to explore other facets of their personality.

Additionally, personality typing systems can reinforce stereotypes and biases. If individuals or groups are associated with specific personality types, it can perpetuate unfair assumptions and discrimination. For example, assuming that introverted individuals are less competent in leadership roles is a stereotype that can be harmful and limiting.

Another criticism of personality typing systems is the potential for individuals to game the system. Some people may answer assessment questions in a way that reflects how they want to be perceived rather than their true personality. This can skew the results and reduce the accuracy of the typing process.

In conclusion, personality typing systems offer valuable insights into human behavior and characteristics, providing structure, practical guidance, and opportunities for self-awareness and personal growth. However, they are not without their weaknesses and limitations. Oversimplification, lack of empirical validation, potential for typecasting, reinforcement of stereotypes, and susceptibility to manipulation are among the drawbacks associated with these systems. It is essential to approach personality typing with a critical and discerning mindset, recognizing their strengths while acknowledging their limitations. Ultimately, the value of personality typing systems lies in their potential to enhance our understanding of ourselves and others, provided we use them thoughtfully and responsibly.

CHAPTER II

Common Types of Challenging Personalities

The narcissist

The term "narcissist" has become increasingly prevalent in contemporary discussions of human behavior and personality. It often describes individuals who exhibit grandiosity, a sense of entitlement, and a pronounced focus on themselves. The concept of narcissism is rooted in Greek mythology, where Narcissus, a character who fell in love with his own reflection, serves as its namesake. In this section, we will delve into the multifaceted nature of narcissism, exploring its characteristics, causes, and the impact it has on individuals and their relationships.

Narcissism can be understood as a personality trait or disorder, with various behaviors and intensities. At one end of the spectrum, narcissistic traits may be relatively common and even adaptive in certain situations. For instance, a healthy level of self-confidence and self-esteem can be advantageous in pursuing one's goals and ambitions. However, when these traits become extreme and maladaptive, they can be indicative of narcissistic personality disorder (NPD).

One of the key characteristics of narcissism is an inflated sense of self-importance and superiority. Narcissists often believe they are exceptionally talented, attractive, or unique and expect special treatment and admiration from others. They may be absorbed with fantasies of power, success, or beauty, and they frequently seek validation and attention to bolster their self-esteem.

Another hallmark of narcissism is a lack of empathy and an inability to consider the feelings and needs of others. Narcissists often exploit and manipulate those around them to fulfill their own desires and maintain their self-image. They may disregard the emotions and boundaries of others, viewing them as secondary to their own needs and desires.

Additionally, narcissists tend to have a fragile self-esteem that is easily wounded. They react defensively to perceived criticism or rejection, often responding with anger, defensiveness, or withdrawal. This hypersensitivity to criticism can make relationships with narcissists challenging, as they may react negatively even to well-intentioned feedback.

The origins of narcissism are complex and multifaceted, with a combination of genetic, environmental, as well as psychological factors contributing to its development. Some researchers suggest that narcissism may have a genetic component, as certain personality traits associated with narcissism may be hereditary. However, environmental factors, such as early childhood experiences, also play a significant role. For example, narcissism may develop as a defense mechanism in response to childhood trauma, neglect, or excessive pampering and indulgence.

In the realm of psychology, narcissism is often viewed through the lens of Sigmund Freud's psychoanalytic theory. According to Freud, narcissism is a normal developmental stage in which individuals direct their love and attention inward, towards themselves. However, in some cases, this stage does not progress, leading to pathological narcissism.

The impact of narcissism on individuals and their relationships can be profound and far-reaching. In their pursuit of self-aggrandizement, narcissists may engage in manipulative behaviors, deceit, and exploitation of others. This can lead to damaged relationships, both personal and professional, as well as legal and ethical consequences. Narcissists may also experience emotional and psychological distress, as their inability to maintain the facade of superiority can result in a constant cycle of seeking external validation.

Recognizing and dealing with narcissism can be challenging. Because narcissists are often charming and charismatic, their true nature may be concealed beneath a veneer of confidence and charisma. However, their behavior patterns may become more apparent over time, and their relationships may deteriorate as others recognize their manipulative tendencies.

Therapeutic approaches to narcissism often involve a combination of psychotherapy and self-reflection. Cognitive-behavioral therapy (CBT) and psychodynamic therapy can help individuals with narcissistic traits gain insight into their behavior, develop healthier coping mechanisms, and work towards greater self-awareness. It is important to note that individuals with narcissistic personality disorder may be resistant to treatment, as they may not perceive a need for change.

In conclusion, narcissism is an intricate and multifaceted personality trait or disorder that involves an exaggerated sense of self-importance, a lack of empathy, and a fragile self-esteem. Its origins are rooted in genetic, environmental, and psychological factors, making it a challenging trait to address and manage. The impact of narcissism on individuals and their relationships can be significant, leading to damaged personal and professional connections. Recognizing and addressing narcissism often requires a combination of therapeutic approaches and self-reflection. Ultimately, understanding the complexities of narcissism is essential for fostering empathy, promoting healthier relationships, and providing support to individuals on the narcissistic spectrum.

The passive-aggressive individual

Passive-aggressiveness is a behavior pattern that can perplex and frustrate those who encounter it. Unlike overt aggression, which is characterized by direct confrontation and hostility, passive-aggression manifests as an indirect and often subtle form of resistance, stubbornness, or non-cooperation. This behavior can undermine relationships, communication, and teamwork, making it essential to understand the passive-aggressive individual, their motivations, and the impact of their actions.

At the heart of passive-aggressiveness lies a conflict between two opposing desires: the need to express dissatisfaction or anger and the fear of confrontation or rejection. Passive-aggressive individuals often struggle with asserting themselves openly due to a fear of conflict or a desire to avoid upsetting others. Instead, they resort to passive means of expressing their discontent or frustration, often confusing their intentions and their targets.

One common manifestation of passive-aggressiveness is the use of sarcasm and subtle insults. Rather than openly expressing their displeasure, passive-aggressive individuals may cloak their criticism in humor or irony. For example, when asked to complete a task they resent, they might respond with a seemingly lighthearted comment that carries a hidden barb. This passive approach allows them to release their frustration while maintaining a veneer of innocence.

Procrastination is another hallmark of passive-aggressive behavior. When faced with tasks they dislike or resent, passive-aggressive individuals may delay or deliberately sabotage their completion. They may offer excuses, blame external factors, or simply fail to follow through on their commitments. This procrastination serves as a way to express their resistance while avoiding direct confrontation or responsibility.

Another common passive-aggressive tactic is the silent treatment or withdrawal of affection. When they are upset or hurt, passive-aggressive individuals may retreat emotionally, refusing to engage in communication or affectionate gestures. This behavior is intended to convey their displeasure without explicitly expressing it, leaving the other party to guess the cause of the sudden emotional distance.

One of the challenges in dealing with passive-aggressive individuals is the difficulty of addressing their behavior. Because they often avoid direct confrontation, bringing the underlying issues to the surface can be challenging. When confronted about their passive-aggressive actions, they may deny any wrongdoing or minimize the significance of their behavior. This can further exacerbate the frustration and confusion of those dealing with them.

The origins of passive-aggressiveness are complex and may be rooted in early life experiences. Some theorists suggest that passive-aggressive behavior may develop in response to environments where open expression of anger or dissatisfaction was discouraged or punished. In such environments, individuals may learn to suppress their feelings and resort to passive means of resistance as a way to cope with their emotions.

Addressing passive-aggressive behavior requires a nuanced approach. Encouraging open and honest communication is essential while acknowledging the individual's fear of conflict or rejection. Providing a secure and non-judgmental space for them where they can express their feelings as well as concerns can be a constructive way to address the underlying issues. Additionally, setting clear expectations and boundaries and holding them accountable for their actions can help curb passive-aggressive tendencies.

In organizational settings, passive-aggressive behavior can be particularly damaging. It can undermine teamwork, hinder productivity, and create a toxic work environment. Managers and leaders need to address passive-aggressive behavior promptly and constructively. This may involve conflict resolution training, creating an open communication culture, and providing channels for employees to express their worries without fear of retaliation.

In conclusion, the passive-aggressive individual represents a subtle and indirect form of conflict that can be challenging to navigate. Their behavior is rooted in a conflict between the desire to express dissatisfaction and the fear of confrontation or rejection. Passive-aggressiveness manifests through sarcasm, procrastination, withdrawal, and other indirect tactics. Understanding the underlying motivations and addressing passive-aggressive behavior through open communication and boundary setting is essential for fostering healthier relationships and productive environments. By unraveling the complexities of passive-aggressiveness, individuals and organizations can work toward more transparent and harmonious interactions.

The manipulator

Manipulation is a behavior that has been observed throughout human history and can take many forms. It involves the subtle or overt influence of others for personal gain, often at the expense of their well-being or interests. Individuals who engage in manipulation are commonly referred to as manipulators. Understanding the manipulator, their tactics, motivations, and the impact of their actions is essential for safeguarding healthy relationships, personal boundaries, and one's own psychological well-being.

Manipulators use various tactics to achieve their goals while concealing their true intentions. One common tactic is guilt-tripping, making others feel responsible or accountable for their actions or emotions. This manipulation technique can be used to elicit compliance or sympathy, effectively placing the burden of their choices on someone else.

Another manipulation tactic is gaslighting, which involves distorting or denying facts, events, or perceptions to make the victim doubt their memory or sanity. Gaslighting can be incredibly disorienting and psychologically damaging, as it erodes an individual's trust in their own judgment and reality.

Emotional manipulation is often characterized by tactics such as playing the victim, using emotional outbursts, or employing passive-aggressive behaviors. Manipulators may feign helplessness or vulnerability to elicit sympathy or assistance while avoiding responsibility for their actions. These tactics can create a cycle of emotional turmoil, making it difficult for victims to disentangle themselves from the manipulator's web.

One of the key motivations behind manipulation is the desire for power and control. Manipulators often seek to dominate or exploit others to fulfill their own needs or desires. Whether it's in personal relationships, professional settings, or social interactions, they aim to gain an upper hand and maintain control over the situation and those involved.

Manipulators may also be driven by a deep-seated insecurity or fear of vulnerability. They use manipulation as a defense mechanism to protect themselves from perceived threats or rejection. By controlling others or maintaining a facade of strength, they attempt to shield their own vulnerabilities and maintain a sense of superiority or invulnerability.

The impact of manipulation on individuals and relationships can be significant and detrimental. Victims of manipulation may experience emotional distress, anxiety, confusion, and a diminished sense of self-worth. Over time, the cumulative effects of manipulation can erode one's self-esteem and self-confidence, making it even more challenging to break free from the manipulator's influence.

Manipulation can also have far-reaching consequences in various aspects of life. In personal relationships, it can lead to toxicity, emotional abuse, and the deterioration of trust and intimacy. In professional settings, manipulative tactics can undermine teamwork, hinder productivity, and create a hostile work environment. Recognizing and addressing manipulation is crucial for protecting one's psychological well-being and fostering healthier interactions.

Dealing with manipulators requires a combination of awareness, assertiveness, and setting boundaries. Recognizing manipulation tactics when they occur is the first step in protecting oneself from their effects. It's essential to trust one's instincts and feelings and not dismiss them when something feels amiss in an interaction.

Setting clear and firm boundaries is another crucial aspect of dealing with manipulators. Establishing and communicating personal boundaries is a way to protect oneself from manipulation and prevent the manipulator from encroaching on one's emotional or psychological space. It may involve stating one's limits, asserting the need for respect, and being willing to disengage from manipulative interactions.

Moreover, seeking support from trusted friends, family members, or professionals can be crucial when dealing with manipulation. Sharing one's experiences and seeking guidance from those who have a more objective perspective can provide validation and clarity. Therapy or counseling can also be valuable for individuals who have experienced manipulation and are struggling with its psychological effects.

In conclusion, the manipulator is a skilled practitioner of psychological control, using various tactics to influence and exploit others for personal gain. Their motivations often stem from a desire for power, control, or a fear of vulnerability. The impact of manipulation can be damaging, leading to emotional distress, erosion of self-esteem, and the deterioration of relationships. Recognizing manipulation, setting boundaries, and seeking support are essential steps in protecting oneself from manipulation's effects and fostering healthier interactions. By understanding the dynamics of manipulation, individuals can empower themselves to navigate manipulative situations more effectively and safeguard their psychological well-being.

The control freak

The term "control freak" is often used colloquially to describe individuals who have an overwhelming need for control in various aspects of their lives. While the phrase may be used lightly, the behavior it represents can be a significant source of stress and conflict in personal and professional relationships. Understanding the control freak, their motivations, tactics, and the consequences of their actions is essential for fostering healthier interactions and maintaining personal boundaries.

Control freaks are characterized by an insatiable need for control and a desire to dictate or influence the behavior and choices of others. They often exhibit perfectionistic tendencies, insisting on high standards and meticulous attention to detail. This need for control can manifest in various domains, including personal relationships, work environments, and social situations.

One common trait of control freaks is the tendency to micromanage. They find it challenging to delegate tasks or trust others to handle responsibilities independently. Instead, they involve themselves in every detail, often creating a sense of suffocation and frustration among those around them.

Control freaks may also engage in intrusive behavior, such as monitoring or questioning the actions and decisions of others. They may pry into personal matters, demand constant updates, or insist on knowing every detail of someone else's life. This behavior is driven by a desire to keep a sense of authority and ensure that their vision or expectations are met.

Control freaks often struggle with flexlbility and adaptability. They may resist change, even when it is necessary or beneficial, and prefer rigid routines and structures. Deviations from their prescribed plan can trigger anxiety or frustration, leading to resistance or conflict.

The motivations behind control freak behavior are complex and may have roots in early life experiences, personality traits, or a fear of loss of control. Some individuals develop a need for control as a response to past trauma or instability, as they seek to create a sense of safety and predictability in their lives. Others may possess personality traits, such as perfectionism or high conscientiousness, that predispose them to seek control.

A desire for power and dominance may also drive control freaks. They derive satisfaction from being in charge and having authority over others, which can boost their self-esteem and sense of importance. The need for control can serve as a coping mechanism for feelings of insecurity or inadequacy, providing a sense of competence and self-assuredness.

The impact of control freak behavior on individuals and relationships can be significant and detrimental. Those subjected to the control of a dominant individual may experience feelings of powerlessness, frustration, and resentment. In personal relationships, the need for control can lead to conflicts, often involving attempts to change or mold the other person to fit the controller's expectations.

In work environments, control freak tendencies can stifle creativity, hinder collaboration, and create a hostile atmosphere. Micromanagement can demoralize employees, reduce job satisfaction, and impede productivity. Control freak behavior can alienate friends and acquaintances in social situations, as others may find it stifling and overbearing.

Addressing control freak behavior requires a combination of self-awareness, assertiveness, and boundary-setting. For the individual exhibiting control freak tendencies, self-reflection and introspection are essential. They must recognize the negative impact of their behavior on themselves and others and be willing to explore the underlying motivations driving their need for control.

Practicing flexibility and letting go of the need for absolute control is a crucial step in managing control freak tendencies. Trusting others, delegating responsibilities, and accepting that not everything can be planned or controlled is vital for personal growth and healthier relationships.

Setting clear and assertive boundaries is essential for those dealing with control freaks. It involves communicating one's need for autonomy and respect while addressing any behavior that feels controlling or intrusive. Constructive dialogue, empathy, and patience can also be valuable tools in navigating relationships with individuals who have control freak tendencies.

In conclusion, the control freak is characterized by an overwhelming need for control and an insatiable desire to influence the behavior and choices of others. Their motivations may stem from a fear of loss of control, a desire for power, or a coping mechanism for insecurity. Control freak behavior can harm relationships, work environments, and social interactions. Recognizing and addressing control freak tendencies through self-awareness, flexibility, and boundary-setting is essential for fostering healthier interactions and maintaining personal autonomy. By understanding the dynamics of control freak behavior, individuals can work toward healthier relationships and personal growth.

The chronic complainer

The chronic complainer is a familiar presence in many social circles and workplaces. These individuals seem to have an unending repertoire of grievances and complaints, whether about their own lives, others' actions, or the state of the world in general. Dealing with chronic complainers can be challenging, as their constant negativity can drain the energy of those around them and create a toxic atmosphere. Understanding the chronic complainer, their motivations, impact, and strategies for coping is crucial for maintaining healthy relationships and personal well-being.

Chronic complainers are defined by their persistent and pervasive habit of voicing dissatisfaction, criticism, and grievances. They often seem incapable of acknowledging positive aspects of situations and tend to focus exclusively on what is wrong, flawed, or unsatisfactory. These complaints can encompass a wide range of topics, from minor inconveniences to major life issues, and may be expressed with varying degrees of intensity.

One key aspect of chronic complainers is their need for attention and validation. By constantly vocalizing their grievances, they seek sympathy, empathy, and acknowledgment from others. Their complaints elicit support and reassurance, often in the form of comforting responses such as, "I'm so sorry you're going through this" or "That sounds really tough."

Another characteristic of chronic complainers is their tendency to externalize blame. Rather than taking responsibility for their circumstances or emotions, they frequently attribute their dissatisfaction to external factors, circumstances, or the actions of others. This externalization allows them to avoid self-reflection and accountability.

The motivations behind chronic complaining can be complex and multifaceted. Some individuals may use complaining as a coping mechanism for dealing with stress, frustration, or feelings of powerlessness. Venting their grievances can provide temporary relief and a sense of catharsis. Others may employ chronic complaining as a way to establish connections and maintain social bonds, using it as a means of initiating conversations and soliciting emotional support.

The impact of chronic complaining on individuals and relationships can be significant. For those on the receiving end of constant complaints, it can be emotionally exhausting and draining. Over time, the negativity of chronic complainers can erode one's own sense of well-being and optimism. Additionally, it can lead to a sense of helplessness or frustration, as attempts to provide solutions or positivity are often met with resistance or further complaints.

Chronic complaining can strain bonds and create a sense of distance in personal relationships. Friends, family members, or partners may find it challenging to maintain empathy and patience when constantly subjected to negativity. This can result in strained relationships and, in some cases, a desire to distance oneself from the chronic complainer.

In work environments, chronic complaining can harm team morale and productivity. The constant negativity can create a toxic atmosphere and hinder collaboration. It may also lead to decreased job satisfaction among coworkers, as the chronic complainer's presence can make the workplace feel more stressful and less enjoyable.

Addressing chronic complaining requires a combination of empathy, assertiveness, and self-care. Self-awareness is the first step toward change for the individual who engages in chronic complaining. They must recognize the impact of their behavior on themselves and others and reflect on the underlying motivations for their complaints. It's crucial to create healthier coping strategies for handling stress and frustration. This may involve practicing mindfulness, seeking professional support, or participating in activities that foster emotional well-being. Learning to express dissatisfaction constructively and engage in problem-solving rather than constant complaining can also lead to personal growth and more positive relationships.

For those dealing with chronic complainers, setting boundaries is crucial. It involves communicating one's need for positivity, assertiveness in addressing excessive complaining, and the willingness to disengage from negative interactions when necessary. Empathetic listening, when appropriate, can provide emotional support without reinforcing chronic complaining.

In conclusion, the chronic complainer is marked by a constant habit of voicing grievances and negativity. Their motivations often include seeking attention, validation, or coping with stress. Chronic complaining can harm relationships and environments, leading to emotional exhaustion and strained connections. Addressing chronic complaining requires self-awareness and healthier coping mechanisms for the complainer, as well as empathy, assertiveness, and boundary-setting for those dealing with chronic complainers. By understanding the dynamics of chronic complaining, individuals can work toward healthier interactions and maintain their own well-being.

The drama queen/king

The term "drama queen" or "drama king" is commonly used to describe individuals who have a penchant for exaggeration, theatrics, and emotional intensity in their interactions and reactions to various situations. These individuals often have a flair for turning everyday occurrences into melodramatic spectacles, drawing attention to themselves and their emotional states. Understanding the drama queen/king, their motivations, tactics, and the impact of their behavior is essential for maintaining healthy relationships and managing the dynamics of emotional intensity.

Drama queens/kings are characterized by their propensity to magnify the significance of events, emotions, or situations. They often exhibit heightened emotional reactions, responding to even minor inconveniences or setbacks with intense displays of anger, frustration, or despair. Everyday challenges are transformed into crises, and they have a knack for attracting attention to their emotional turmoil.

One key element of the drama queen/king's behavior is their need for validation and reassurance. By exaggerating their emotional reactions and creating dramatic scenarios, they seek sympathy, empathy, and acknowledgment from others. Their dramatic outbursts often prompt responses such as, "Are you okay?" or "What happened?" These responses provide them with the attention and support they crave.

Another tactic that drama queens/kings commonly employs is sensational language and gestures. They may describe their experiences in highly dramatic terms, using phrases like "It's the end of the world" or "I can't take it anymore." These exaggerated expressions are designed to elicit strong emotional responses from others, drawing them into the drama.

The motivations behind drama queen/king behavior can be complex and multifaceted. Some individuals may use drama to cope with overwhelming emotions or stress. The heightened intensity of their reactions may provide temporary relief and catharsis. Others may seek attention and affirmation of their significance, using dramatic displays to maintain the focus on themselves and their emotions.

The impact of drama queen/king behavior on individuals and relationships can be significant. Those who are close to drama queens/kings often find themselves caught up in the emotional whirlwind, forced to navigate the turbulent waters of exaggerated reactions and intense emotions. This can be emotionally exhausting and draining, as individuals attempt to provide support and validation in the face of constant drama.

In personal relationships, drama queen/king behavior can strain bonds and create a sense of volatility. Friends, family members, or partners may find it challenging to maintain emotional equilibrium when subjected to dramatic displays' constant ups and downs. This can lead to frustration, resentment, and, in some cases, a desire to distance oneself from the drama.

In work environments, drama queen/king tendencies can create disruptions, impact team dynamics, and hinder productivity. The constant need for attention and emotional intensity can develop a toxic atmosphere, making it difficult for coworkers to focus on their tasks and maintain a positive work environment.

Addressing drama queen/king behavior requires a combination of empathy, assertiveness, and boundary-setting. Self-awareness is the first step toward change for the individual who exhibits dramatic tendencies. They must recognize the impact of their behavior on themselves and others and reflect on the underlying motivations for their dramatic displays.

Developing healthier coping mechanisms for managing emotions and stress is crucial. This may involve practicing emotional regulation techniques, seeking professional support, or participating in activities that promote emotional well-being. Learning to express emotions authentically without resorting to exaggeration or theatrics can lead to personal growth and more balanced interactions.

For those dealing with drama queens/kings, setting boundaries is essential. It involves communicating one's need for emotional stability, assertiveness in addressing excessive drama, and the willingness to disengage from dramatic interactions when necessary. Empathy and support can be provided without reinforcing the drama, helping individuals maintain healthier relationships and personal well-being.

In conclusion, the drama queen/king is characterized by their tendency to exaggerate emotions and create melodramatic scenarios. Their motivations often include seeking attention, validation, or coping with overwhelming emotions. Drama queen/king behavior can significantly impact relationships and environments, leading to emotional exhaustion and strained connections. Addressing this behavior requires self-awareness, healthier coping mechanisms, and setting boundaries for the individuals who exhibit dramatic tendencies, as well as empathy, assertiveness, and boundary-setting for those dealing with drama queens/kings. By understanding the dynamics of dramatic behavior, individuals can work toward healthier interactions and emotional equilibrium.

The pessimist

Pessimism is a perspective characterized by a consistently negative outlook on life and a belief that unfavorable outcomes are more likely than favorable ones. Pessimists tend to focus on the dark side of situations, expecting the worst, and often struggle to see the silver lining. While some degree of caution and skepticism can be healthy, chronic pessimism can have far-reaching effects on an individual's emotional and mental well-being, as well as their relationships and the overall quality of life. Understanding the pessimist, their motivations, thought patterns, and the impact of their worldview is essential for fostering empathy and finding ways to cope with this outlook.

Pessimists approach life with a fundamental expectation of negative outcomes. They often anticipate problems, setbacks, and disappointments, even in situations where optimism would prevail. This negative orientation can manifest in various aspects of their lives, from personal relationships to professional endeavors.

One of the key characteristics of pessimists is their tendency to engage in catastrophic thinking. They have a knack for magnifying the potential consequences of negative events, assuming the worst-case scenario is not only possible but inevitable. This cognitive distortion often leads to anxiety and excessive worry, as pessimists constantly ruminate on the dire implications of their fears.

Another hallmark of pessimism is focusing on past failures and disappointments. Pessimists frequently use these past experiences as evidence to support their negative outlook on the future. They may dwell on their mistakes and view them as a reflection of their inherent incompetence or unworthiness.

The motivations behind pessimism are complex and can vary from person to person. Some individuals may adopt a pessimistic outlook as a defense mechanism against disappointment. By expecting the worst, they believe they are better prepared to handle setbacks when they occur. Others may have learned pessimism from their upbringing or from role models who exhibited a similarly negative worldview.

Pessimism can also be fueled by low self-esteem and a lack of self-confidence. Individuals who doubt their abilities or self-worth may find it difficult to envision positive outcomes for themselves. Pessimism becomes a self-fulfilling prophecy, as their negative beliefs undermine their motivation and efforts.

The impact of chronic pessimism on individuals and relationships can be profound. Pessimists often experience higher levels of stress, anxiety, and depression. Constantly anticipating negative events can lead to a perpetual state of unease and emotional turmoil. In personal relationships, pessimism can strain bonds and create a sense of hopelessness, as friends and loved ones may struggle to provide reassurance and support.

In professional settings, pessimism can hinder productivity and limit opportunities for growth. Pessimistic employees may be less likely to take risks, seize new opportunities, or pursue ambitious goals due to their fear of failure and negative expectations. This can limit their career advancement and job satisfaction.

Coping with pessimism requires a combination of empathy, support, and cognitive-behavioral strategies. Self-awareness is the first step toward change for the individual who struggles with chronic pessimism. Recognizing the impact of their negative beliefs on their mental and emotional well-being is essential. Cognitive-behavioral therapy (CBT) can be valuable for challenging and reframing pessimistic thought patterns. It helps individuals identify and replace negative cognitive distortions with more realistic and constructive beliefs.

Developing a gratitude practice can also be beneficial for pessimists. Cultivating an awareness of positive aspects in life and regularly expressing gratitude for them can gradually shift one's focus away from constant negativity. Additionally, engaging in mindfulness or relaxation techniques can help reduce anxiety and rumination.

For those in relationships with pessimists, empathy and patience are essential. Understanding that pessimism is not a deliberate choice but often a deeply ingrained habit can foster compassion. Encouraging open communication and providing emotional support can help pessimists feel less isolated and more understood.

In conclusion, the pessimist is characterized by a consistently negative outlook on life, anticipating unfavorable outcomes and dwelling on past failures. Various motivations, including a fear of disappointment and low self-esteem can fuel pessimism. Chronic pessimism can have significant negative effects on mental and emotional well-being, relationships, and career opportunities. Coping with pessimism requires self-awareness, cognitive-behavioral strategies, and a supportive environment that promotes empathy and understanding. By understanding the complexities of pessimism, individuals can work toward more balanced and positive perspectives on life.

The know-it-all

The term "know-it-all" is often used to describe individuals who exude an air of unwavering confidence and a belief that they have superior knowledge or expertise on various topics. While confidence and knowledge are generally positive traits, the know-it-all takes them to an extreme, often monopolizing conversations, dismissing alternative viewpoints, and displaying a lack of humility. Understanding the know-it- all, their motivations, communication style, and the impact of their behavior is essential for maintaining constructive interactions and fostering open dialogue.

Know-it-alls are characterized by their tendency to assert their expertise or knowledge on virtually any subject, often without regard for the accuracy or relevance of their statements. They frequently interject in conversations, offering unsolicited advice or information, and may be condescending or dismissive of others' contributions. This behavior stems from an underlying belief in their intellectual superiority and a need to establish their dominance in discussions.

One key aspect of know-it-alls is their lack of receptivity to alternative perspectives or information that contradicts their own beliefs. They may exhibit confirmation bias, seeking out information that supports their pre-existing views and dismissing or ignoring data that challenges them. This intellectual rigidity can hinder constructive dialogue and inhibit personal growth.

Another characteristic of know-it-alls is their propensity to offer solutions or advice, even when it is not solicited. They may believe they always know what is best for others and assume a paternalistic or patronizing tone in their interactions. This can be particularly irksome to those who value autonomy and prefer making their own decisions.

The motivations behind know-it-all behavior can be complex and multifaceted. Some individuals adopt this approach as a defense mechanism to mask feelings of insecurity or inadequacy. They hope to shield themselves from criticism or rejection by projecting an image of infallibility. Others may have a deep-seated need for validation and admiration, seeking to impress others with their apparent expertise.

A desire for control or dominance in social interactions may also drive know-it-alls. They view conversations as opportunities to assert their authority and establish themselves as the ultimate authority on a given topic. This can create power dynamics in relationships and make it challenging for others to engage in equitable dialogue. The impact of know-it-all behavior on individuals and relationships can be significant. Those who interact with know-it-alls may feel frustrated, belittled, or disrespected. Constant asserting expertise and dismissing others' contributions can erode self-esteem and create a hostile or intimidating environment.

In personal relationships, know-it-alls may struggle to maintain meaningful connections, as their need to be right or to control conversations can alienate friends, family members, or partners. In professional settings, know-it-all tendencies can hinder collaboration, reduce morale, and create a sense of division among coworkers. Addressing know-it-all behavior requires a combination of self-awareness, empathy, and communication skills. Self-reflection is the first step toward change for the individual who exhibits know-it-all tendencies. Recognizing the impact of their behavior on themselves and others and examining the underlying motivations for their need to dominate conversations is essential.

Developing humility and receptivity to alternative viewpoints is crucial. This may involve actively listening to others, acknowledging the limits of one's knowledge, and being willing to admit when one is wrong. Practicing empathy and respecting others' autonomy in decision-making can also help foster more balanced interactions.

For those dealing with know-it-alls, assertiveness and communication skills are valuable tools. Setting boundaries by calmly and respectfully asserting the need for open dialogue and mutual respect can help create a more constructive atmosphere. It may also involve diplomatically challenging inaccuracies or biases when appropriate.

In conclusion, the know-it-all is characterized by unwavering confidence and a belief in their intellectual superiority. Their motivations may include a desire for validation, control, or a defense mechanism against insecurity. Know-it-all behavior can have significant negative effects on relationships and interactions, as it can create frustration and inhibit constructive dialogue. Addressing this behavior requires self-awareness, humility, and effective communication skills for both the individuals who exhibit know-it-all tendencies and those dealing with them. By understanding the complexities of know-it-all behavior, individuals can work toward more balanced and respectful interactions.

The silent and withdrawn

Silence can be a effective form of communication, but when it becomes a default mode of interaction, it can be indicative of deeper issues. The silent and withdrawn individual is often characterized by their reticence, hesitancy to engage in social interactions, and preference for solitude. This behavior can raise concerns about their well-being and can be puzzling to those who care about them. Understanding the silent and withdrawn, their motivations, challenges, and the impact of their behavior is essential for fostering empathy, offering support, and facilitating their reconnection with the world.

Silent and withdrawn individuals tend to limit verbal communication and may remain silent in social settings. They often appear reserved, introverted, or shy and may hesitate to initiate or sustain conversations. While some degree of introversion is normal and healthy, an extreme preference for solitude and silence can indicate underlying struggles.

One characteristic of the silent and withdrawn is their avoidance of social interactions or situations that involve group activities. They may decline invitations to social gatherings, prefer solitary activities, or limit their interactions to a small circle of trusted individuals. This preference for isolation can be a coping mechanism for managing social anxiety or discomfort.

Another aspect of silent and withdrawn behavior is the difficulty in expressing emotions or thoughts verbally. Even when conversing, they may struggle to articulate their feelings or engage in small talk. This difficulty in verbal expression can create a sense of isolation and disconnect from others.

The motivations behind silent and withdrawn behavior are varied and complex. Some individuals may be introverted by nature, finding solace and comfort in solitude. Others may have experienced past trauma or difficult social experiences that have led them to retreat from the social world as a means of self-protection. In some cases, silent and withdrawn behavior may be a manifestation of social anxiety or depression, making social interactions overwhelming or emotionally taxing.

The impact of chronic silence and withdrawal on individuals can be profound. Silent and withdrawn individuals may experience feelings of loneliness, isolation, and disconnection from the world. The absence of social engagement can lead to a sense of being misunderstood or overlooked, which can exacerbate feelings of alienation. Over time, this isolation can negatively affect mental and emotional well-being.

In personal relationships, silent and withdrawn behavior can create challenges for communication and connection. Loved ones may feel frustrated or hurt by the lack of verbal expression and may struggle to comprehend the underlying reasons for the individual's withdrawal. In professional settings, this behavior can hinder teamwork, limit career opportunities, and create challenges in networking or collaboration.

Addressing silent and withdrawn behavior requires a combination of empathy, support, and understanding. For the silent and withdrawn individual, self-awareness is the first step toward change. Recognizing the impact of their behavior on themselves and their relationships is essential. Identifying the motivations behind their withdrawal, whether it be anxiety, past trauma, or a simple preference for solitude, can provide valuable insights.

Developing strategies for managing social anxiety or discomfort is crucial. This may entail seeking professional help, such as therapy or counseling, to solve underlying emotional issues. Building social skills and gradually increasing exposure to social situations can also help individuals become more comfortable with interaction.

Patience and empathy are vital for those in relationships with silent and withdrawn individuals. Understanding that silent and withdrawn behavior is not a personal rejection but often a reflection of internal struggles can foster compassion. Providing emotional support and creating a secure and non-judgmental space for communication can help silent and withdrawn individuals feel more comfortable expressing themselves.

In conclusion, the silent and withdrawn individual is characterized by their preference for solitude and reticence in social interactions. Their behavior may be rooted in various motivations, including introversion, social anxiety, past trauma, or personal preference. Chronic silence and withdrawal can have significant negative effects on mental and emotional well-being, relationships, and career opportunities. Addressing this behavior requires self-awareness, support, and understanding for both the individuals who are silent and withdrawn and those who care about them. By understanding the complexities of silent and withdrawn behavior, individuals can work toward reconnection and healthier relationships with the world around them.

The overly competitive

Competition is a natural and often healthy aspect of human interaction. It can motivate individuals to work for excellence, push their limits, and achieve their goals. However, when competition becomes excessive and all-consuming, it can result in unfavorable consequences for the individuals involved and the environments they inhabit. The overly competitive individual is characterized by an unrelenting drive to win at all costs, often to the detriment of others and their own well-being. Understanding the overly competitive, their motivations, behaviors, and the impact of their approach is essential for fostering a balanced perspective on competition and maintaining positive relationships.

Overly competitive individuals approach competition with an insatiable desire to win and a relentless focus on outcomes. They may engage in any activity or context—from sports and academics to professional and personal relationships—to emerge as the victor. This singular focus on winning can lead them to disregard ethical considerations, fair play, and the well-being of others.

One hallmark of the overly competitive is their inability to accept defeat gracefully. Losing, even in minor or inconsequential situations, can be deeply distressing for them. They may respond to defeat with anger, frustration, or denial, often refusing to acknowledge their shortcomings or the superior performance of others.

Another characteristic of overly competitive individuals is their constant comparison of themselves to others. They measure their worth and success in relation to their competitors, and their self-esteem is often contingent on outperforming or surpassing others. This constant need for external validation can create a sense of insecurity and anxiety.

The motivations behind overly competitive behavior can vary widely. Some individuals may be driven by a fear of failure, perfectionism, or a desire to prove their worth to themselves or others. Others may have been conditioned from a young age to prioritize winning and success above all else, whether by parental pressure or societal expectations.

Competition can be a double-edged sword. On one hand, it can inspire growth, innovation, and the pursuit of excellence. On the other hand, excessive competitiveness can lead to negative consequences. In personal relationships, overly competitive individuals may alienate friends and loved ones, as their need to win can overshadow empathy, cooperation, and emotional connection. In professional settings, they may create toxic environments where winning becomes the sole focus, undermining teamwork and collaboration. Moreover, overly competitive individuals may experience significant stress, anxiety, and burnout. Their relentless pursuit of success can lead to physical and mental health issues, as they often sacrifice self-care and well-being in their quest for victory. The inability to accept defeat gracefully can also hinder personal growth and resilience.

Balancing ambition and healthy competition requires self-awareness, perspective, and a commitment to ethical values. For the overly competitive individual, self- reflection is the first step toward change. Recognizing the impact of their behavior on themselves and others is essential. Understanding that winning is not the only measure of success and that growth and learning can come from failure is crucial.

Resilience and a growth mindset are two things that can help change the emphasis from winning to improving oneself. Competition can be viewed more positively if one embraces the idea that obstacles and failures are chances for growth and learning.

For those in relationships with overly competitive individuals, assertiveness and communication skills are essential. Setting boundaries by calmly and respectfully asserting the need for ethical behavior and fair play can help develop a more positive and collaborative atmosphere. Encouraging self-reflection and supporting the development of a healthier approach to competition can also be valuable.

In conclusion, the overly competitive individual is characterized by an unrelenting drive to win at all costs, often to the detriment of others and their own well-being. Their motivations may include a fear of failure, perfectionism, or a desire for external validation. Excessive competitiveness can negatively affect personal relationships, emotional well-being, and the overall quality of life. Balancing ambition and competition requires self-awareness, perspective, and a commitment to ethical values for both the overly competitive individuals and those who interact with them. By understanding the complexities of competitiveness, individuals can work toward a healthier and more balanced approach to competition and success.

CHAPTER III

The Psychology Behind Challenging Behaviors

The role of upbringing and experiences

Challenging behaviors, whether they manifest as excessive competitiveness, chronic complaining, or withdrawal, are often shaped by a complex interplay of psychological, environmental, and experiential factors. Among these factors, upbringing and life experiences play a significant and foundational role. Understanding how one's upbringing and life experiences contribute to the development of challenging behaviors is essential for promoting self-awareness, empathy, and effective strategies for personal growth and behavior modification.

The early years of life are critical in shaping an individual's behavioral patterns and coping mechanisms. Upbringing, encompassing parenting styles, familial dynamics, and early life experiences, lays the foundation for how individuals perceive the world, themselves, and their relationships. Parenting styles, in particular, have a profound impact on the development of challenging behaviors.

Children raised in environments characterized by excessive control, neglect, or inconsistency may develop coping mechanisms that manifest as challenging behaviors in adulthood. For example, individuals who experienced overbearing or authoritarian parenting may develop tendencies toward defiance, rebellion, or a need for excessive control in response to early experiences of oppression or lack of autonomy. Conversely, those who grew up in neglectful or permissive environments may exhibit challenging behaviors stemming from a lack of structure, discipline, or guidance in their formative years.

A person's behavior and psychological health can also be permanently impacted by traumatic events that occurred during childhood or adolescence. Experiences such as abuse, loss, or witnessing significant adversity can contribute to the development of challenging behaviors as individuals grapple with the emotional aftermath of these events. For instance, individuals who endured emotional or physical abuse may exhibit chronic complaining or withdrawal as ways to cope with unresolved trauma or emotional pain.

Furthermore, the quality of early attachments and relationships can significantly influence an individual's ability to form healthy connections and manage challenging behaviors. Secure attachments during childhood can foster emotional resilience and the development of effective communication and coping skills. In contrast, insecure or disrupted attachments may lead to difficulties in regulating emotions and navigating interpersonal relationships, which can contribute to challenging behaviors.

Life experiences beyond childhood, such as relationships, career setbacks, or personal crises, also play a pivotal role in shaping behavior. Traumatic events or ongoing stressors can trigger maladaptive coping mechanisms that manifest as challenging behaviors. For example, individuals facing chronic stress in their careers may resort to excessive competitiveness as a way to assert control and alleviate feelings of inadequacy or anxiety.

Moreover, societal and cultural influences can impact the development of challenging behaviors. Cultural norms and expectations may shape one's beliefs about success, interpersonal relationships, and emotional expression.

Individuals from cultures that emphasize competition and achievement, for instance, may be more prone to overly competitive behaviors.

Understanding the role of upbringing and life experiences in challenging behaviors is the first step toward personal growth and behavior modification. Self-awareness is crucial in recognizing how early experiences and traumas may have influenced one's current behavior patterns. Seeking therapy or counseling can offer a safe space to explore and process these experiences, facilitating healing and the development of healthier coping strategies.

For those dealing with individuals exhibiting challenging behaviors rooted in their upbringing and life experiences, empathy and support are key. Recognizing that challenging behaviors may be a response to past traumas or coping mechanisms developed in challenging environments can foster compassion. Encouraging individuals to seek professional help and offering a supportive environment for their growth and healing can be invaluable.

In conclusion, the role of upbringing and life experiences is a foundational component in understanding the psychology behind challenging behaviors. Early life experiences, parenting styles, traumatic events, and cultural influences all shape an individual's coping mechanisms and behavior patterns. Recognizing the impact of these factors is essential for fostering self-awareness, empathy, and effective strategies for personal growth and behavior modification. By understanding the complex interplay of upbringing and life experiences, individuals can work toward healthier and more adaptive responses to life's challenges.

The influence of biology and genetics

Challenging behaviors, ranging from chronic complaining to excessive competitiveness, are often the product of intricate interactions between biological, genetic, psychological, and environmental factors. While upbringing and experiences significantly shape an individual's behavior, the influence of biology and genetics is equally profound. Understanding how an individual's genetic makeup and neurobiological processes contribute to the development of challenging behaviors is essential for gaining insight into the underlying causes and potential avenues for intervention and support.

Genetics plays a substantial role in shaping an individual's predisposition to certain behaviors. While no single gene is responsible for any specific challenging behavior, genetics can contribute to one's susceptibility. For example, studies have suggested that genes associated with mood regulation and impulsivity, such as those related to serotonin and dopamine neurotransmitters, may influence behaviors like chronic complaining or emotional instability. Genetic factors can influence an individual's temperament, emotional reactivity, and response to stress, which in turn can contribute to the development of challenging behaviors.

Family history and genetic predisposition can also play a role in challenging behaviors. Individuals with a known family history of mental health disorders, addiction, or behavioral issues may be at a heightened risk due to genetic inheritance. While genetics alone does not determine behavior, it can create a vulnerability that interacts with environmental factors to influence the development of challenging behaviors.

In addition to genetic factors, the neurobiological underpinnings of behavior provide valuable insights into challenging behaviors. The brain's structure, functioning, and neurotransmitter systems play a significant role in shaping an individual's responses and behaviors. For instance, chronic complainers may exhibit differences in the brain regions connected with emotional processing and regulation, contributing to their propensity for negativity and dissatisfaction.

Moreover, the role of neurotransmitters like serotonin and dopamine in mood regulation and reward processing can influence behaviors like excessive competitiveness. Individuals with variations in these neurotransmitter systems may seek out competitive situations as a means of achieving the pleasurable feelings associated with winning, contributing to their overly competitive behavior.

The influence of biology and genetics on challenging behaviors is further compounded by the interaction between nature and nurture. Genetic predispositions can be modulated by environmental factors, such as early life experiences, trauma, and stress. For example, an individual with a genetic vulnerability to anxiety may be more likely to develop anxiety-related behaviors if they experience a traumatic event during their upbringing. Having a knowledge of the role of genetics and biology in challenging behaviors can have important implications for intervention and support. While genetics may contribute to one's susceptibility to challenging behaviors, it does not determine the outcome. The interplay between genetic and environmental factors underscores the potential for targeted interventions and preventive measures.

For individuals dealing with challenging behaviors rooted in genetics and biology, seeking professional help can be invaluable. Mental health professionals can conduct assessments to identify underlying genetic vulnerabilities and neurobiological factors contributing to behavior. This information can inform treatment approaches, which may include medication, therapy, or behavioral interventions tailored to address the specific biological and genetic influences.

Additionally, for individuals with a family history of challenging behaviors, genetic counseling can provide valuable insights into potential risks and strategies for prevention. Genetic counselors can offer guidance on family planning decisions, lifestyle modifications, and early intervention strategies to mitigate the impact of genetic predispositions.

In conclusion, the influence of biology and genetics is a significant component of the psychology behind challenging behaviors. Genetic predispositions and neurobiological processes can contribute to an individual's susceptibility to behaviors like chronic complaining, excessive competitiveness, or emotional instability. Understanding the intricate interplay between genetics as well as environmental factors is essential for tailoring interventions and support for individuals dealing with challenging behaviors. By recognizing the role of biology and genetics, individuals and professionals can work together to solve the underlying causes and foster healthier behavioral responses.

Coping mechanisms and defense mechanisms

Challenging behaviors, whether they manifest as passive-aggressiveness, manipulation, or excessive competitiveness, often serve as adaptive responses to the complex interplay of psychological, environmental, and experiential factors. Central to the psychology behind these behaviors are coping mechanisms and defense mechanisms, which individuals employ to navigate the challenges and stresses of life. Understanding how these mechanisms influence behavior is crucial for unraveling the underlying causes of challenging behaviors and promoting healthier alternatives for managing stress and adversity.

Coping mechanisms encompass a wide range of strategies and techniques that individuals employ to manage stress, emotions, and difficult situations. These mechanisms can be adaptive or maladaptive, according on their effectiveness in promoting emotional well-being and problem-solving. In the context of challenging behaviors, an individual's choice of coping mechanisms can significantly influence their behavior and interpersonal interactions.

For example, an individual who resorts to chronic complaining as a coping mechanism may use this behavior as a means of seeking attention and emotional support. Chronic complainers often use their complaints to express frustration, sadness, or anxiety, and they may hope that others will validate their feelings and offer comfort. While this coping mechanism may provide temporary relief, it can become a challenging behavior when it is used excessively and disruptively in social or professional settings.

Similarly, passive-aggressive behavior can be seen as a coping mechanism for individuals who struggle with assertiveness and direct communication. Instead of openly expressing their needs, concerns, or frustrations, they may resort to indirect and often subtle forms of resistance or hostility. Passive-aggressiveness can serve as a way to avoid confrontation and maintain a sense of control, but it can create challenges in interpersonal relationships when it leads to misunderstandings and resentment.

Defense mechanisms, on the other hand, are psychological strategies that individuals unconsciously employ to protect themselves from uncomfortable thoughts, feelings, or situations. While defense mechanisms can serve as protective shields against psychological distress, they can also give rise to challenging behaviors when they distort perceptions, hinder self-awareness, and impede constructive problem-solving.

For instance, denial is a common defense mechanism employed to protect oneself from acknowledging uncomfortable truths or realities. In the context of challenging behaviors, an individual in denial may refuse to accept the consequences of their actions or the impact of their behavior on others. This can lead to a absence of accountability and hinder personal growth and behavioral change.

Projection is another defense mechanism that can contribute to challenging behaviors. Individuals who engage in projection may unconsciously attribute their own unacceptable thoughts, feelings, or behaviors to others. For example, a manipulative individual may accuse others of being manipulative or deceitful, deflecting attention away from their own behavior. This projection can create confusion and conflict in relationships.

Understanding the role of coping and defense mechanisms in challenging behaviors requires a nuanced approach. It involves recognizing that these mechanisms, while intended to serve as protective or adaptive strategies, can become problematic when used excessively or inappropriately. Self-awareness is a crucial first step for individuals who wish to address their challenging behaviors and explore healthier alternatives.

For individuals dealing with challenging behaviors in themselves or others, empathy and communication are essential. Recognizing that challenging behaviors may be a manifestation of underlying stress, emotions, or unmet needs can foster compassion and open the door to productive dialogue. Encouraging individuals to explore and adopt healthier coping mechanisms, such as mindfulness, assertiveness, or problem-solving skills, can be valuable in promoting more adaptive responses to challenges.

In conclusion, coping mechanisms and defense mechanisms are integral components of the psychology behind challenging behaviors. Coping mechanisms represent a broad range of strategies individuals use to manage stress and emotions, while defense mechanisms serve as protective shields against psychological distress. When these mechanisms are employed excessively or inappropriately, they can give rise to challenging behaviors that disrupt interpersonal relationships and hinder personal growth. Recognizing the role of these mechanisms in behavior is essential for fostering self-awareness, empathy, and effective strategies for managing challenging behaviors. By understanding the complexities of coping and defense mechanisms, individuals can work toward healthier and more adaptive responses to life's challenges.

Emotional intelligence and self-awareness

Challenging behaviors, whether they manifest as passive-aggressiveness, manipulation, or chronic complaining, often have their roots in complex psychological dynamics. One crucial aspect of understanding and addressing these behaviors is the role of emotional intelligence and self-awareness. Emotional intelligence, which encompasses the capacity to recognize, comprehend, manage, and navigate one's own and others' emotions, plays a pivotal role in shaping behavior. Additionally, self-awareness, the capacity to reflect upon and understand one's own thoughts, feelings, and motivations, is a cornerstone of emotional intelligence and a key factor in addressing and modifying challenging behaviors.

Emotional intelligence, often called EQ, involves several interrelated components that are pertinent to challenging behaviors. One of these components is emotional recognition, which is the ability to accurately perceive and determine emotions in oneself and others. Individuals with high emotional intelligence can decipher the emotions underlying their own behavior and the behavior of those around them. This recognition is fundamental in addressing challenging behaviors, as it provides insight into the emotional triggers and motivations behind such actions.

For instance, an individual who exhibits passive-aggressive behavior may not overtly express their anger or frustration. Instead, they may rely on subtle, indirect expressions of hostility. Emotional intelligence allows observers to recognize the underlying anger or resentment, even when it is not explicitly communicated. This recognition is a critical step toward understanding the root causes of the behavior.

Another component of emotional intelligence is emotional understanding, which involves the ability to comprehend the complexities of emotions, including their causes and consequences. This understanding allows individuals to empathize with others, recognizing that challenging behaviors often emerge from emotional struggles, past traumas, or unmet needs.

Empathy, a key aspect of emotional understanding, plays a pivotal role in addressing challenging behaviors. It enables individuals to connect with the emotions of others, fostering a sense of compassion and a willingness to understand their perspective. When dealing with someone who engages in manipulation or chronic complaining, empathizing with their underlying emotional pain or insecurities can facilitate more constructive and empathetic responses.

Emotional management is another critical component of emotional intelligence. It involves the capacity to regulate one's own emotions and reactions effectively. Individuals with high emotional intelligence can manage their emotions in a healthy and adaptive manner, even in challenging situations. This ability is crucial in addressing challenging behaviors, as it allows individuals to respond calmly and empathetically rather than reacting defensively or aggressively.

Self-awareness is closely intertwined with emotional intelligence and serves as its foundation. It involves the capacity to introspectively examine one's thoughts, feelings, and motivations. Self-aware individuals possess a deeper understanding of their own emotional triggers, vulnerabilities, and patterns of behavior. This self-examination is instrumental in addressing and modifying challenging behaviors.

For those who exhibit challenging behaviors, self-awareness is the first step toward change. Recognizing the impact of their behavior on themselves and others and understanding the emotional motivations behind their actions is essential. Self-awareness enable individuals to identify patterns of behavior, triggers, and underlying emotional struggles that contribute to challenging behaviors.

Furthermore, self-awareness is instrumental in fostering personal growth and behavioral modification. It allows individuals to take ownership of their actions, acknowledge areas for improvement, and seek help or support when needed. Individuals who possess self-awareness are more likely to engage in introspection, therapy, or counseling to address the root causes of their challenging behaviors.

In personal and professional relationships, emotional intelligence and self-awareness are essential for navigating and resolving conflicts related to challenging behaviors. Individuals who possess high emotional intelligence can approach these situations with empathy as well as a genuine desire to understand the emotions and perspectives of others. This can lead to more productive and compassionate interactions, even in the face of challenging behaviors.

In conclusion, emotional intelligence and self-awareness are pivotal factors in understanding and addressing challenging behaviors. Emotional intelligence encompasses the capacity to recognize, understand, manage, and navigate emotions in oneself and others. Self-awareness involves introspection and a deeper understanding of one's own thoughts, feelings, and motivations. These qualities provide valuable insights into the emotional triggers and motivations behind challenging behaviors, allowing for more empathetic and effective responses. By fostering emotional intelligence and self-awareness, individuals can work toward healthier and more adaptive ways of coping with and expressing their emotions.

The impact of trauma and past relationships

Challenging behaviors, which can range from passive-aggressiveness to manipulation or excessive competitiveness, often have deep-seated roots in an individual's life experiences, particularly in the realm of trauma and past relationships. Understanding the role of trauma and past relationships is crucial for unraveling the complex psychological dynamics that drive these behaviors. Traumatic experiences and unhealthy relationship patterns can significantly shape an individual's behavior, emotional responses, and coping mechanisms, shedding light on why challenging behaviors manifest and persist.

Trauma, whether it stems from childhood experiences, accidents, abuse, or other distressing events, can leave profound imprints on an individual's psyche. Trauma disrupts one's sense of safety and security, often triggering a fight-or-flight response that can become chronic and maladaptive over time. Challenging behaviors can serve as coping mechanisms developed in response to past trauma, as individuals seek ways to manage the overwhelming emotions, distressing memories, and a sense of powerlessness that trauma can evoke.

For example, individuals who have experienced emotional or physical abuse in childhood may exhibit passive-aggressive behaviors as a means of protecting themselves from further harm. Passive-aggressiveness allows them to express their anger or frustration indirectly, reducing the risk of retaliation. This behavior pattern can become ingrained as a survival strategy, even when the threat of abuse is no longer present, leading to ongoing challenging behaviors in adult relationships.

Similarly, individuals who have survived traumatic events may develop manipulation as a coping mechanism for regaining a sense of control. Manipulation can involve tactics such as deceit, guilt-tripping, or emotional blackmail, as individuals use these strategies to navigate relationships and situations that evoke feelings of vulnerability or helplessness. While manipulation may offer temporary relief, it can damage trust and create conflict in relationships, perpetuating challenging behaviors.

Past relationships also play a significant role in shaping an individual's behavior and emotional responses. Unhealthy relationship dynamics, such as codependency, toxic patterns of communication, or abuse, can become templates for future interactions. Individuals who have experienced unhealthy relationships may carry these patterns into new relationships, perpetuating challenging behaviors and creating cycles of dysfunction.

For example, an individual who grew up witnessing a parent engage in chronic complaining may adopt this behavior as a way of seeking attention and validation in their adult relationships. They may unconsciously replicate the pattern of chronic complaining they observed in childhood, perpetuating the cycle of challenging behavior in their own relationships.

Moreover, past relationships can influence an individual's attachment style, which in turn shapes their behavior in subsequent relationships. People with anxious or avoidant attachment styles may display problematic behaviors which arise from their incapacity to trust others, their fear of being abandoned, or their inability to experience emotional closeness. These behaviors can create obstacles to forming healthy, fulfilling relationships and contribute to interpersonal conflict.

Understanding the impact of trauma and past relationships on challenging behaviors requires a nuanced and compassionate approach. For individuals exhibiting these behaviors, recognizing the connection between past experiences and current behavior patterns is an essential first step toward change. Trauma-informed therapy, which acknowledges the role of trauma in shaping behavior and focuses on healing and recovery, can be instrumental in addressing the underlying emotional wounds and developing healthier coping strategies.

In personal and professional relationships, empathy and communication are vital when dealing with individuals who exhibit challenging behaviors rooted in trauma or past relationships. Recognizing that these behaviors may be a response to unresolved emotional pain, fear, or insecurity can foster compassion and patience. Encouraging individuals to seek therapeutic support and providing a supportive environment for healing can be invaluable.

In conclusion, the impact of trauma and past relationships is a significant factor in understanding the psychology behind challenging behaviors. Traumatic experiences and unhealthy relationship patterns can significantly shape an individual's behavior, emotional responses, and coping mechanisms. Recognizing the connection between past experiences and current behavior is essential for fostering self-awareness, empathy, and effective strategies for addressing and modifying challenging behaviors. By addressing the underlying emotional wounds and patterns of behavior, individuals can work toward healthier and more adaptive ways of navigating relationships and managing emotions.

CHAPTER IV

Strategies for Effective Communication

Active listening

Effective communication is a cornerstone of building and maintaining healthy relationships, and when it comes to dealing with challenging behaviors, it becomes even more crucial. Challenging behaviors, which can range from passive-aggressiveness to chronic complaining or manipulation, often stem from underlying emotional or psychological issues. To address and understand these behaviors, one of the most powerful tools is active listening. Active listening is a communication tactic that involves not only hearing words but also comprehending and empathizing with the speaker's thoughts, feelings, and perspectives. It is a foundational strategy for fostering understanding, de-escalating conflicts, and building trust with individuals exhibiting challenging behaviors.

Active listening begins with the intention to fully engage with the speaker and genuinely understand their point of view. It requires setting aside one's own judgments, assumptions, and agenda to create a safe and open space for communication. When individuals feel heard and validated, they will likely share their thoughts and feelings honestly, even if they are struggling with challenging behaviors.

One crucial aspect of active listening is giving the speaker your full attention. In a world filled with distractions, this can be a powerful signal that you value and respect the speaker's perspective. It involves making eye contact, facing the speaker, and providing verbal and non-verbal cues, such as nodding or using affirmative words like "I see" or "I understand," to show that you are actively participated in the conversation.

Additionally, active listening involves avoiding interruptions and allowing the speaker to express themselves fully. Challenging behaviors often emerge from unmet needs, emotional distress, or a sense of not being heard. When individuals are given the space to articulate their thoughts and feelings without interruption, it can lead to a sense of relief as well as empowerment.

Empathy is a central component of active listening. Empathizing with the speaker means not only understanding their perspective but also sharing in their emotional experience to some extent. It involves recognizing and acknowledging the speaker's emotions and showing that you care about their well-being. Empathy can be a powerful tool for de-escalating conflicts and building trust, as it communicates that you are willing to connect with the speaker on an emotional level.

Reflective listening is another technique within active listening that involves paraphrasing or summarizing what the speaker has said to make sure that you have understood their message accurately. This technique helps clarify any potential misunderstandings and provides an opportunity for the speaker to confirm or clarify their message. It also conveys to the speaker that you are genuinely interested in understanding their perspective.

Active listening is particularly beneficial when dealing with challenging behaviors, as it allows individuals to express their underlying emotions and concerns. For example, an individual who engages in chronic complaining may be seeking validation, empathy, or a solution to an unresolved issue. Active listening can help uncover the root causes of the complaining behavior and provide a platform for addressing those underlying needs.

In situations involving manipulation, active listening can be a powerful tool for exposing hidden agendas and fostering transparency. By actively engaging with the manipulator and seeking to understand their motivations, individuals can encourage open and honest communication. This can help prevent further manipulation and promote more authentic interactions.

Furthermore, active listening can de-escalate conflicts that may arise from challenging behaviors. When individuals feel heard and understood, they are less likely to become defensive or confrontational. Instead, they are more inclined to engage in constructive problem-solving and resolution.

In personal and professional relationships, active listening is essential for establishing trust and rapport with individuals exhibiting challenging behaviors. It communicates respect, empathy, and a genuine desire to understand their perspectives. Active listening can also create an environment where individuals feel secure to share their concerns and work collaboratively toward solutions.

In conclusion, active listening is a fundamental strategy for effective communication with individuals exhibiting challenging behaviors. It involves giving the speaker your full attention, avoiding interruptions, empathizing with their emotions, and practicing reflective listening. Active listening creates a safe and open space for individuals to express their thoughts as well as emotions, which is crucial for understanding the underlying causes of challenging behaviors and promoting healthier interactions. By employing active listening techniques, individuals can build trust, de-escalate conflicts, and foster more empathetic and constructive communication with those who exhibit challenging behaviors.

Non-verbal communication

Effective communication is a complex skill that goes beyond the spoken or written word. When dealing with challenging behaviors, such as passive-aggressiveness, manipulation, or excessive competitiveness, the role of non-verbal communication cannot be overstated. Non-verbal cues, including facial expressions, body language, gestures, and tone of voice, carry powerful messages and can either enhance or hinder communication. Understanding and leveraging non-verbal communication is a key strategy for fostering understanding, de- escalating conflicts, and building rapport with individuals exhibiting challenging behaviors.

Facial expressions are a primary channel of non-verbal communication. The human face is incredibly expressive, capable of conveying an array of emotions, from joy and empathy to anger and frustration. When dealing with individuals exhibiting challenging behaviors, paying close attention to their facial expressions can provide valuable insights into their emotional state and underlying motivations.

For example, an individual who is chronically complaining may exhibit facial expressions of discontent, frustration, or dissatisfaction. These expressions can signal their emotional distress and dissatisfaction with their current situation or circumstances. Recognizing these cues can prompt a more empathetic and understanding response, as it communicates that you are attuned to their emotional experience.

Body language is another critical component of non-verbal communication. Posture, gestures, and movements can convey a wealth of information about an individual's thoughts, feelings, and intentions. When dealing with challenging behaviors, observing and interpreting body language can help uncover underlying emotions and motivations.

In situations involving excessive competitiveness, individuals may display tense body language, such as clenched fists, a rigid posture, or intense eye contact. These cues can signal their intense desire to win or assert dominance. Understanding these non-verbal cues can inform your response, allowing you to address their competitive drive in a more constructive and empathetic manner.

Tone of voice is yet another powerful non-verbal communication tool. The way words are spoken—whether with warmth and empathy or with irritation and impatience—can drastically impact the message's reception. Individuals exhibiting challenging behaviors often react strongly to the tone of voice used in communication.

For instance, when dealing with manipulative behavior, individuals may employ a soothing or persuasive tone to influence others. Recognizing this tone can help individuals respond assertively and maintain boundaries. Conversely, responding with an equally calm and assertive tone can convey confidence and reduce the manipulator's attempts to control the situation.

Furthermore, non-verbal communication includes elements like eye contact and personal space. Maintaining appropriate eye contact can convey sincerity, interest, and confidence, while excessive or insufficient eye contact can signal discomfort or avoidance. Understanding cultural and individual differences in the use of personal space is also crucial, as invading someone's personal space can be perceived as invasive and threatening.

Non-verbal communication is particularly valuable when dealing with passive-aggressive behaviors. Passive-aggressive individuals often struggle with direct communication, and their non-verbal cues may provide clues to their underlying emotions and intentions. Recognizing signs of discomfort or tension in their body language can prompt a more empathetic and direct conversation about their concerns or frustrations.

Moreover, non-verbal communication can be instrumental in de-escalating conflicts related to challenging behaviors. When individuals perceive that you are attuned to their non-verbal cues and are responding with empathy and understanding, it can reduce defensiveness and promote more open and productive communication.

In personal and professional relationships, leveraging non-verbal communication can help individuals establish trust and rapport with those exhibiting challenging behaviors. It conveys respect, empathy, and a willingness to understand the unspoken messages behind the behavior. By honing their ability to read and respond to non-verbal cues effectively, individuals can navigate challenging situations with greater sensitivity and effectiveness.

In conclusion, non-verbal communication is a powerful strategy for effective communication with individuals exhibiting challenging behaviors. It encompasses facial expressions, body language, gestures, tone of voice, and other cues that convey emotions and intentions. Understanding and responding to these non-verbal cues can provide valuable insights into the emotional state and motivations of individuals with challenging behaviors. By leveraging non-verbal communication effectively, individuals can foster understanding, de-escalate conflicts, and build rapport with those they are communicating with, ultimately promoting more empathetic and constructive interactions.

Empathy and perspective-taking

Empathy and perspective-taking are profound and transformative strategies in the realm of effective communication, especially when dealing with challenging behaviors. Empathy, often described as the capacity to comprehend and share the feelings of another, forms the bedrock of compassionate communication. Perspective-taking, on the other hand, involves putting oneself in another person's shoes, attempting to understand their thoughts, emotions, and motivations. These strategies are essential for fostering understanding, de-escalating conflicts, and building connections with individuals exhibiting challenging behaviors.

Empathy serves as a powerful tool for establishing rapport and trust with individuals displaying challenging behaviors. It involves not only recognizing the emotions that others are experiencing but also genuinely connecting with those emotions. When individuals feel that their feelings are understood and acknowledged, they are more likely to open up and engage in more constructive and honest communication.

For example, when dealing with someone who exhibits passive-aggressive behavior, empathizing with their underlying frustration or hurt can create a bridge for understanding. Recognizing that passive-aggressive behaviors often stem from a reluctance to express anger directly, due to fear of conflict or perceived consequences, allows for a more empathetic and less confrontational approach.

Empathy can also be instrumental in addressing manipulation. Manipulative behaviors often emerge from deep-seated insecurities, unmet needs, or a desire for control. By empathizing with the manipulator's emotional vulnerabilities and acknowledging their underlying pain or insecurity, individuals can foster a more empathetic and less adversarial conversation. This approach opens the door to addressing the root causes of manipulation and finding healthier ways to meet their emotional needs.

Perspective-taking complements empathy by allowing individuals to see the world through another's eyes. It involves the willingness to step outside of one's own perspective and consider the thoughts, feelings, and motivations of the person exhibiting challenging behaviors. Perspective-taking can be particularly valuable when dealing with individuals who struggle to express themselves directly or verbally.

In situations involving excessive competitiveness, for instance, perspective-taking can help individuals understand the competitive individual's drive for success or recognition. It allows them to see the world from the competitive person's point of view and recognize that their behavior may stem from a desire to prove themselves or attain a sense of self-worth. This understanding can result in a more empathetic and constructive responses that address the individual's emotional needs.

Furthermore, perspective-taking can be a vital strategy for de-escalating conflicts related to challenging behaviors. When individuals make a genuine effort to understand the motivations and emotions behind the behavior, it can diffuse tension and develop an environment conducive to problem-solving and resolution. This approach shifts the focus from blame and judgment to understanding and collaboration.

In personal and professional relationships, empathy and perspective-taking are essential for building connections with individuals exhibiting challenging behaviors. They convey respect, a willingness to understand, and a commitment to fostering positive interactions. When individuals practice empathy and perspective-taking, they are more likely to establish trust as well as rapport with those they are communicating with, even in challenging situations.

Empathy and perspective-taking also promote active listening, as individuals must be fully engaged in the communication process to genuinely understand the emotions and perspectives of others. Active listening, combined with empathy and perspective-taking, creates a dynamic and effective communication strategy that fosters understanding and mutual respect.

In conclusion, empathy and perspective-taking are powerful strategies for effective communication with individuals exhibiting challenging behaviors. These strategies involve understanding and connecting with the emotions and perspectives of others, even when those emotions are challenging or uncomfortable. By practicing empathy and perspective-taking, individuals can build trust, de-escalate conflicts, and foster connections with those they are communicating with, ultimately promoting more empathetic and constructive interactions.

Assertiveness vs. aggression

Effective communication is a foundation of healthy relationships, and when dealing with challenging behaviors, understanding the distinction between assertiveness and aggression becomes paramount. Assertiveness and aggression represent two distinct communication styles with vastly different outcomes. While assertiveness promotes respectful and constructive interactions, aggression often leads to conflict and resistance. In the context of challenging behaviors, mastering the art of assertiveness is a key strategy for fostering understanding, resolving conflicts, and promoting healthier communication.

Assertiveness is a communication style characterized by the ability to express one's thoughts, feelings, needs, and boundaries clearly and respectfully. Assertive individuals are confident in expressing themselves without being domineering or disrespectful of others' perspectives. When dealing with challenging behaviors, assertiveness is a powerful tool for setting boundaries, addressing concerns, and promoting understanding.

For example, when confronting passive-aggressive behavior, assertiveness allows individuals to express their feelings and concerns directly and respectfully. Instead of resorting to aggression or passive avoidance, assertive individuals can address the issue at hand while maintaining a constructive and empathetic tone. This approach conveys that their feelings and concerns are valid and that they expect a respectful and direct response.

In situations involving manipulation, assertiveness empowers individuals to assert their own needs and boundaries firmly and without aggression. Manipulative individuals may attempt to guilt-trip, deceive, or control others, but assertiveness allows individuals to respond confidently and assert their autonomy. They can communicate that they are not willing to be manipulated while still acknowledging the manipulator's emotions or concerns.

Moreover, assertiveness is a valuable strategy for de-escalating conflicts related to challenging behaviors. It involves active listening, expressing oneself clearly, and seeking mutual understanding. When individuals approach conflicts assertively, they are more likely to engage in constructive problem-solving and resolution, rather than escalating the situation through aggression or defensiveness.

On the other hand, aggression is a communication style characterized by hostility, intimidation, and a disregard for the feelings or perspectives of others. Aggressive individuals seek to dominate or control others through fear, anger, or forceful tactics. When dealing with challenging behaviors, responding with aggression can exacerbate conflicts and hinder understanding.

For example, responding to chronic complaining with aggression, such as yelling or name-calling, is likely to escalate the situation further. Instead of addressing the underlying issues, aggression creates a hostile environment that impedes effective communication and perpetuates negative emotions.

Similarly, responding to manipulation with aggression can lead to power struggles and resistance. Aggressive responses may cause the manipulator to become defensive or escalate their tactics, further complicating the situation. In contrast, assertiveness allows individuals to assert their boundaries and needs firmly but respectfully, reducing the likelihood of an aggressive escalation.

Understanding the distinction between assertiveness and aggression is essential for building and maintaining healthy relationships, especially when dealing with individuals exhibiting challenging behaviors. Assertiveness conveys self-confidence, respect for others, and a commitment to open and respectful communication. It promotes understanding, resolution, and mutual respect.

In contrast, aggression undermines trust, fosters defensiveness, and hinders productive communication. It can perpetuate conflicts, damage relationships, and lead to further challenges in dealing with challenging behaviors. Recognizing the negative impact of aggression and choosing assertiveness as a communication style is a critical step toward fostering healthier interactions.

In personal and professional relationships, individuals can benefit from honing their assertiveness skills and practicing respectful and direct communication. This approach promotes understanding, sets clear boundaries, and fosters an environment conducive to addressing and resolving challenging behaviors.

In conclusion, assertiveness versus aggression is a pivotal distinction in effective communication when dealing with challenging behaviors. Assertiveness empowers individuals to express themselves clearly and respectfully, set boundaries, and seek mutual understanding. In contrast, aggression creates hostility, escalates conflicts, and hinders productive communication. By mastering the art of assertiveness, individuals can navigate challenging behaviors with confidence, empathy, and the ability to foster healthier communication and relationships.

Managing emotional reactions

Dealing with challenging behaviors, whether they manifest as passive-aggressiveness, manipulation, or chronic complaining, can be emotionally taxing. In such situations, the ability to manage one's emotional reactions becomes a pivotal strategy for effective communication. Emotions can run high, and uncontrolled reactions may exacerbate conflicts or hinder understanding. Learning to manage emotional responses is essential for fostering empathy, promoting constructive communication, and resolving issues when confronted with challenging behaviors.

One of the first steps in managing emotional reactions is self-awareness. Recognizing and acknowledging one's own emotional responses to challenging behaviors is crucial. When individuals encounter behaviors that trigger frustration, irritation, or anger, it is essential to pause and reflect on their emotional state before responding. This self-awareness enable individuals to identify their emotional triggers and choose more deliberate and constructive responses.

For instance, when faced with chronic complaining, individuals may feel annoyance or impatience. Recognizing these emotions is the first step toward managing them effectively. Instead of reacting impulsively or defensively, self-awareness enables individuals to pause, take a deep breath, and respond with greater patience and empathy.

Emotional regulation is another critical aspect of managing emotional reactions. It involves the ability to control and modulate emotional responses in challenging situations. Emotional regulation allows individuals to remain composed and focused on the issue at hand, rather than becoming entangled in emotional turmoil. In situations involving manipulation, emotional regulation is particularly valuable. Manipulative behaviors can provoke feelings of anger, betrayal, or frustration. Emotional regulation empowers individuals to maintain a calm and composed demeanor, which can prevent the manipulator from achieving their desired outcomes. It also allows individuals to respond rationally and assertively, rather than reacting emotionally or impulsively.

Furthermore, empathy plays a significant role in managing emotional reactions. Empathy entails recognizing and understanding the emotions and perspectives of others. When individuals encounter challenging behaviors, responding with empathy can help de-escalate conflicts and promote understanding. For example, when dealing with passive-aggressive behavior, it can be challenging to maintain empathy. Passive-aggressiveness can be frustrating, as it often involves indirect communication and veiled hostility. However, responding with empathy involves recognizing that passive-aggressive individuals may be struggling with assertiveness or fear of confrontation. It acknowledges their emotional state and seeks to understand their perspective, fostering a more constructive and empathetic response.

Additionally, problem-solving and solution-focused thinking are instrumental in managing emotional reactions effectively. Instead of dwelling on negative emotions or becoming embroiled in conflicts, individuals can channel their energy toward finding practical solutions to the issues at hand. This approach shifts the focus from emotional reactions to constructive problem-solving.

In situations involving excessive competitiveness, for instance, individuals may feel threatened or provoked. Managing emotional reactions in such scenarios involves shifting the focus from competition to collaboration. Encouraging a problem-solving approach that seeks mutually beneficial outcomes can reduce tension and promote understanding.

Moreover, active listening is an integral part of managing emotional reactions. Active listening includes not only hearing the words spoken but also comprehending the underlying emotions and motivations. When individuals actively listen to those exhibiting challenging behaviors, it demonstrates respect, empathy, and a commitment to understanding their perspective.

In personal and professional relationships, managing emotional reactions is essential for effective communication when dealing with challenging behaviors. It allows individuals to respond with empathy, patience, and assertiveness, rather than reacting emotionally or defensively. By practicing self-awareness, emotional regulation, empathy, problem-solving, and active listening, individuals can navigate challenging behaviors with greater composure, empathy, and the ability to foster constructive communication and resolution.

In conclusion, managing emotional reactions is a crucial strategy for effective communication when dealing with challenging behaviors. It involves self-awareness, emotional regulation, empathy, problem-solving, and active listening. These components empower individuals to respond with composure, empathy, and constructive communication, even in emotionally charged situations. By mastering the art of managing emotional reactions, individuals can navigate challenging behaviors with patience, understanding, and the ability to foster healthier interactions and relationships.

CHAPTER V

Conflict Resolution Techniques

The importance of conflict resolution

Human interaction will inevitably lead to conflict because of differences in needs, expectations, values, and opinions. Although conflict can be difficult and uncomfortable, it also offers a chance for development, better relationships, and constructive change. The process of confronting and settling disagreements or conflicts is known as conflict resolution, and it is essential to preserving harmony in both personal and professional contexts. Understanding the importance of conflict resolution is essential for fostering healthy relationships, facilitating collaboration, and promoting constructive change.

First and foremost, conflict resolution is critical for maintaining healthy relationships. Unresolved conflicts can fester and erode trust, communication, and emotional bonds. In personal relationships, such as those with family members, friends, or romantic partners, unresolved conflicts can lead to resentment and distance. In professional settings, conflicts left unaddressed can hinder teamwork, productivity, and job satisfaction. By actively engaging in conflict resolution, individuals can repair and strengthen their relationships, fostering trust, mutual respect, and open communication.

Furthermore, conflict resolution is vital for fostering collaboration and problem-solving. In group or team settings, disagreements are bound to arise as diverse perspectives and ideas collide. Effective conflict resolution enables groups to navigate these differences, harnessing the unique strengths and insights of each member. It encourages individuals to listen actively, consider alternative viewpoints, and work together toward shared goals. In this way, conflict resolution transforms conflicts into opportunities for innovation, creativity, and improved decision-making.

Moreover, conflict resolution promotes personal growth and self-awareness. When individuals engage in conflict resolution, they are prompted to reflect on their own thoughts, feelings, and behaviors. This introspection permits them to gain insight into their own values, triggers, and communication patterns. Conflict resolution challenges individuals to confront their biases, assumptions, and emotional reactions, fostering self-awareness and personal development. It offers a chance for individuals to learn from their experiences and become more resilient as well as adaptable in the face of future conflicts.

Conflict resolution also contributes to a more peaceful and harmonious society. In communities and nations, unresolved conflicts can escalate into violence, civil unrest, or even war. Effective conflict resolution processes, such as mediation, negotiation, or diplomacy, provide peaceful alternatives to violence and allow conflicting parties to find mutually acceptable solutions. These processes can prevent the destructive consequences of unresolved conflicts, promote social cohesion, and facilitate the establishment of just and equitable societies.

Moreover, conflict resolution is crucial in the workplace for promoting a healthy and productive environment. Conflicts that go unresolved can lead to tension, stress, and decreased job satisfaction among employees. In contrast, when organizations prioritize conflict resolution, they create a culture of openness, trust, as well as accountability. Employees feel empowered to voice their concerns, seek assistance in resolving conflicts, and contribute to a more positive and collaborative work environment. This, in turn, can enhance job satisfaction, employee retention, and overall organizational success.

In personal relationships, conflict resolution fosters emotional intimacy and connection. Conflict can be an opportunity for individuals to express their feelings, needs, and vulnerabilities to one another. When couples or family members engage in constructive conflict resolution, they not only resolve the immediate issue but also deepen their understanding of each other's perspectives and emotions. This process can lead to increased trust, empathy, and a stronger emotional bond.

Furthermore, conflict resolution enhances communication skills. Effective conflict resolution requires active listening, assertiveness, empathy, and the capacity to express oneself clearly and respectfully. By honing these communication skills, individuals can improve their relationships, navigate conflicts more effectively, and become more persuasive and influential communicators in various aspects of their lives.

In conclusion, conflict resolution is of paramount importance for fostering harmony, growth, and positive change in personal, professional, and societal contexts. It enables individuals to maintain healthy relationships, promote collaboration and problem-solving, foster personal development and self-awareness, and contribute to a more peaceful and harmonious world. People and communities can gain a great deal from respectfully and productively resolving conflicts when they acknowledge its significance and actively participate in constructive conflict resolution processes.

Collaborative problem-solving

Conflict is an inevitable part of human interaction, arising from differences in opinions, values, needs, and expectations. In navigating these conflicts, the art of collaborative problem-solving has emerged as a vital conflict resolution technique. Collaborative problem-solving involves individuals or groups working together to find mutually satisfactory solutions to complex issues. This approach emphasizes active communication, creativity, and a commitment to win-win outcomes. Understanding the principles and benefits of collaborative problem-solving is essential for fostering cooperation, resolving conflicts, and achieving positive outcomes in various personal, professional, and societal contexts.

Collaborative problem-solving is rooted in the recognition that many challenges and opportunities require diverse perspectives and expertise for effective resolution. In a collaborative process, individuals from various backgrounds, disciplines, and experiences come together to pool their insights, knowledge, and skills. This diversity of thought often leads to more creative and holistic problem-solving approaches.

One of the key principles of collaborative problem-solving is the pursuit of win-win solutions. This approach focuses on finding solutions that satisfy the interests and needs of each party, rather than promoting a zero-sum mentality where one party's gain is another's loss. Win-win negotiation promotes cooperation and collaboration, fostering positive relationships and long-term partnerships.

Collaborative problem-solving also encourages a growth mindset, where individuals view difficulties as opportunities for learning and improvement. In a collaborative setting, individuals are more willing to experiment, to take risks, and learn from both successes as well as failures. This mindset fosters resilience, adaptability, and a willingness to continuously refine and enhance problem-solving approaches.

Furthermore, collaborative problem-solving promotes personal and professional growth. When individuals engage in collaborative problem-solving, they are prompted to reflect on their own thoughts, feelings, and behaviors. This introspection permits them to gain insight into their own values, triggers, and communication patterns. Collaborative problem-solving challenges individuals to confront their biases, assumptions, and emotional reactions, fostering self-awareness and personal development.

Moreover, collaborative problem-solving often leads to more innovative solutions. When individuals from diverse backgrounds and disciplines come together, they bring unique perspectives and concepts to the table. This diversity of thought sparks creativity and can result in novel approaches that may not have emerged through individual problem-solving efforts. Innovation is further fostered when participants challenge assumptions, explore unconventional solutions, and engage in collective brainstorming.

In professional settings, collaborative problem-solving is particularly valuable for addressing complex challenges that require a multidisciplinary approach. Cross-functional teams, that includes individuals with diverse skills and expertise, can tackle intricate problems more effectively. Collaborative problem-solving also promotes a sense of ownership and buy-in among team members, leading to more successful implementation of solutions.

Furthermore, in personal relationships, collaborative problem-solving enhances communication and teamwork. Couples, families, and friends who engage in collaborative problem-solving are better equipped to navigate conflicts, address shared challenges, and make important decisions together. Collaborative problem-solving encourages mutual respect, active listening, and a commitment to finding win-win solutions.

In societal contexts, collaborative problem-solving is essential for addressing intricate issues such as climate change, public health crises, and social justice concerns. These challenges often require collaboration among governments, organizations, communities, and individuals from diverse backgrounds. Collaborative problem-solving approaches, such as consensus-building and multi-stakeholder engagement, are essential for creating meaningful and lasting solutions to these global challenges.

In conclusion, collaborative problem-solving is a powerful conflict resolution technique that emphasizes cooperation, creativity, and a commitment to win-win outcomes. It recognizes the significance of diverse perspectives and expertise in tackling complex issues. Collaborative problem-solving fosters personal and professional growth, innovation, and effective resolution in various personal, professional, and societal contexts. By recognizing the principles and benefits of collaborative problem-solving, individuals and communities can work together to find an innovative and efficient solutions to the challenges they face, ultimately building bridges to resolution and positive change.

Negotiation and compromise

Negotiation and compromise are two integral components of effective conflict resolution and problem-solving in personal, professional, and societal contexts. They are essential skills that allow individuals and groups to navigate differences, find common ground, and reach mutually satisfactory outcomes. Negotiation involves the process of discussing and bargaining with the goal of reaching an agreement, while compromise entails making concessions to accommodate the interests and needs of all parties involved. Understanding the principles and significance of negotiation and compromise is fundamental for fostering cooperation, resolving conflicts, and achieving positive outcomes.

Negotiation is a dynamic and interactive process that occurs when individuals or parties with differing interests come together to find a mutually acceptable solution. Effective negotiation involves active listening, clear communication, and a willingness to engage in problem-solving. It begins by identifying the interests, concerns, and priorities of each party, which helps frame the negotiation and guide the search for common ground. One of the key principles of negotiation is the pursuit of win-win solutions, where all parties benefit from the agreement. This approach focuses on finding solutions that satisfy the interests and needs of each party, rather than promoting a zero-sum mentality where one party's gain is another's loss. Win-win negotiation promotes cooperation and collaboration, fostering positive relationships and long-term partnerships. Negotiation also involves a degree of assertiveness and advocacy for one's own interests and needs. Individuals participating in a negotiation should clearly and respectfully express their positions and preferences. However, it is equally important to balance assertiveness with active listening and empathy for the perspectives and needs of others. This balance is essential for creating an atmosphere of mutual respect and understanding during the negotiation process.

Moreover, negotiation often requires flexibility and adaptability. As discussions progress, individuals may need to reevaluate their initial positions and explore alternative solutions. Negotiation is a dynamic process where creative problem-solving and brainstorming can lead to innovative solutions that may not have been apparent initially. The ability to adapt and explore new options is essential for finding mutually satisfactory outcomes.

Compromise, on the other hand, is closely related to negotiation and involves making concessions to reach an agreement. Compromise recognizes that not all parties can achieve their ideal outcomes, and it requires a willingness to find middle ground and prioritize the collective interest over individual desires. While compromise may involve giving up something of value, it also fosters cooperation, goodwill, and resolution. Compromise is a valuable strategy for conflict resolution in personal relationships. In couples, families, or friendships, individuals often have differing needs, preferences, or expectations. Compromise allows them to find solutions that accommodate each other's concerns and reach mutually acceptable agreements. It promotes emotional closeness and teamwork, enhancing the quality of relationships.
In professional settings, compromise is essential for addressing conflicting interests and finding common ground. It is often used in negotiations over contracts, project timelines, or resource allocation. Effective compromise fosters a collaborative work environment, where individuals are willing to make concessions to achieve shared goals and objectives. It also demonstrates flexibility and adaptability, key attributes in today's rapidly changing business landscape.

Furthermore, in societal contexts, compromise plays a pivotal role in governance and decision-making. Democratic processes often involve negotiation and compromise among diverse stakeholders to formulate policies and laws that reflect the interests and values of the entire population. Compromise is essential for maintaining social stability, upholding the rule of law, and accommodating the needs and perspectives of different segments of society.

It is important to note that negotiation and compromise do not imply weakness or capitulation. Instead, they represent a pragmatic and principled approach to conflict resolution that recognizes the complexity of human interactions and the importance of finding common ground. Skilled negotiators and compromisers understand the balance between advocating for their own interests and being open to the perspectives and needs of others.

In conclusion, negotiation and compromise are fundamental components of effective conflict resolution and problem-solving. They involve active listening, clear communication, and a willingness to engage in problem-solving to find mutually satisfactory solutions. Negotiation emphasizes win-win outcomes and assertiveness, while compromise entails making concessions to accommodate the interests and needs of all parties. These skills are crucial in personal, professional, and societal contexts, fostering cooperation, resolving conflicts, and achieving positive outcomes. By recognizing the principles and significance of negotiation and compromise, individuals and communities can build bridges to resolution and create a more harmonious and cooperative world.

Mediation and third-party intervention

Mediation and third-party intervention are valuable processes in conflict resolution that involve the assistance of a neutral facilitator to help disputing parties find mutually acceptable solutions. These approaches are particularly effective when conflicts are complex, emotionally charged, or resistant to resolution through direct negotiations. Mediation entails the use of a trained mediator who guides the parties in reaching their own agreement, while third-party intervention may include arbitration or adjudication where the neutral party makes a decision. Both processes offer advantages in personal, professional, and societal contexts, as they promote effective communication, empower participants, and contribute to lasting resolutions.

Mediation is a collaborative and voluntary process in which a mediator facilitates communication between disputing parties. The mediator, who is neutral and impartial, helps the parties identify their underlying interests, concerns, and priorities. Through open dialogue and active listening, the mediator assists in reframing the issues and generating creative solutions. Mediation empowers the parties to build their own agreement, promoting a sense of ownership and commitment to the outcome.

One of the key benefits of mediation is its ability to enhance communication between parties in conflict. In many disputes, breakdowns in communication contribute to the escalation and perpetuation of the conflict. Mediation offers a structured and safe environment for participants to express their feelings, thoughts, and needs while ensuring that they are heard and understood by the other party. This open and respectful dialogue fosters empathy and understanding, helping individuals see the issue from multiple perspectives.

Moreover, mediation is well-suited for conflicts involving emotional or interpersonal dynamics. In personal relationships, such as family disputes or neighborly conflicts, emotions often run high and can hinder direct negotiations. Mediation offers a supportive and constructive space for addressing these issues. By encouraging empathy and cooperation, it can help participants find common ground and rebuild relationships.

In professional settings, workplace conflicts, such as disputes between employees or contract disagreements, can disrupt productivity and morale. Mediation offers a confidential and non-adversarial process for resolving these conflicts. It allows employees or business partners to address their concerns and collaboratively develop solutions that benefit all parties. This approach can lead to improved working relationships and organizational harmony.

Furthermore, in societal contexts, mediation can play a vital role in addressing community disputes or larger social conflicts. Community mediators facilitate dialogue and negotiation among stakeholders, helping them find common ground and reach agreements that benefit the community as a whole. Mediation is also used in international diplomacy and conflict resolution, where neutral mediators facilitate negotiations between nations to prevent or resolve conflicts without resorting to violence.

Third-party intervention, which encompasses arbitration and adjudication, provides another avenue for resolving conflicts when direct negotiations are unproductive or parties cannot reach an agreement on their own. In arbitration, a neutral third party reviews the evidence and arguments presented by both sides and makes a binding decision. Adjudication involves a similar process but may occur in a formal legal setting, with a judge or tribunal rendering a decision.

One of the advantages of third-party intervention is that it provides a definitive resolution to a conflict. In cases where parties are unable or unwilling to reach a compromise, the decision of the neutral third party can provide closure and finality. This can be particularly valuable in legal disputes or contractual disagreements where clarity and enforcement of the resolution are crucial.

Additionally, third-party intervention can expedite conflict resolution. The formal nature of the process often results in a quicker resolution compared to lengthy court proceedings. This efficiency can save parties time and resources and help them move forward with their lives or business activities.

However, it's important to note that third-party intervention may not always be the preferred method, especially when parties prioritize maintaining control over the outcome and are willing to engage in dialogue and compromise. Mediation offers more flexibility and empowers participants to shape the resolution themselves, which can lead to more satisfying and sustainable outcomes in some cases.

In conclusion, mediation and third-party intervention are powerful tools for facilitating constructive conflict resolution in various contexts. Mediation promotes effective communication, empathy, and collaboration among participants, empowering them to reach mutually acceptable solutions. Third-party intervention, including arbitration and adjudication, offers definitive resolutions and can expedite the process when direct negotiations are unproductive. By recognizing the advantages and limitations of these processes, individuals and communities can choose the approach that best suits their needs and contribute to the achievement of lasting and harmonious resolutions.

Setting boundaries

Conflict is a natural part of human interactions, arising from differences in opinions, values, and expectations. Effective conflict resolution techniques are essential for maintaining healthy relationships and promoting constructive communication. Among these techniques, setting boundaries stands out as a crucial tool for resolving conflicts while maintaining personal well-being and mutual respect. Boundaries, in the context of conflict resolution, are the limits and guidelines individuals establish to protect their emotional, physical, and mental health while respecting the needs and boundaries of others. Understanding how to set and communicate boundaries is fundamental for fostering healthier relationships and achieving constructive conflict resolution.

One of the key functions of setting boundaries in conflict resolution is to protect one's well-being. Boundaries enable individuals to identify and communicate what they consider acceptable and unacceptable behavior from others. For example, in a romantic relationship, setting boundaries may involve establishing limits on personal space, privacy, or acceptable forms of communication. In a workplace, boundaries can define working hours, acceptable treatment by colleagues or superiors, and what tasks or responsibilities an individual is willing to take on.

Furthermore, setting boundaries promotes self-care and emotional well-being. It empowers individuals to prioritize their own needs, values, and feelings, which is essential for maintaining a healthy sense of self-esteem and self-worth. When individuals set and enforce boundaries, they send a clear message that they value and respect themselves. This sense of self-worth can enhance overall emotional well-being, contributing to increased self-confidence and resilience in the face of conflicts.

Effective boundary setting involves assertiveness, which is the ability to express one's thoughts, feelings, and needs clearly and respectfully. Assertiveness allows individuals to communicate their boundaries with confidence, without aggression or passivity. It conveys that their needs and values are valid and deserving of respect. When individuals practice assertive boundary setting, they are more likely to be understood and respected by others.

In personal relationships, setting boundaries can lead to improved communication and reduced conflicts. For example, in a friendship, if one friend consistently cancels plans at the last minute, the other friend may set a boundary by expressing that they value reliability and expect more notice for cancellations. This boundary can lead to more considerate behavior and less frustration in the friendship.

Moreover, setting boundaries is crucial for maintaining autonomy and individuality within relationships. In close relationships, such as partnerships or family dynamics, it is common for boundaries to blur, leading to a loss of personal space and identity. Effective boundary setting helps individuals maintain their independence and self-expression, which is essential for personal growth and fulfillment.

In professional settings, boundaries are essential for maintaining a healthy work-life balance. The ability to set clear boundaries around work hours, expectations, and personal time is crucial for preventing burnout and maintaining overall well-being. Setting boundaries at work can also promote better time management and increased productivity, as individuals are more likely to focus on tasks when they have dedicated time for work and leisure.

However, it is essential to recognize that boundary setting is a dynamic process that may require ongoing adjustment and negotiation. As individuals and relationships evolve, so do their needs and boundaries. Effective boundary setting involves open and honest communication with others about changing needs and expectations.

Furthermore, setting boundaries is not solely about protecting oneself; it also involves respecting the boundaries of others. Mutual respect for each other's boundaries is the foundation of healthy and respectful relationships. It involves active listening, empathy, and a commitment to understanding and accommodating the needs and limits of others.

In conflict resolution, setting boundaries can be a proactive strategy to prevent conflicts from escalating. For example, if two coworkers frequently clash over differing work styles, one of them may decide to set a boundary by explaining their preferred work methods and requesting that their coworker respect these preferences. This proactive approach can help avoid conflicts from arising in the first place by clarifying expectations and fostering mutual respect.

Setting boundaries can also be a valuable tool for resolving conflicts that have already arisen. When conflicts occur, individuals can communicate their boundaries to the other party, explaining what behavior or actions are causing distress and what changes they would like to see. By doing so assertively and respectfully, individuals create a constructive framework for discussing and resolving the conflict.

In conclusion, setting boundaries is a powerful conflict resolution technique that empowers healthy relationships and fosters constructive communication. It serves to protect one's well-being, promote self-care, and maintain autonomy within relationships. Effective boundary setting involves assertiveness, clear communication, and mutual respect for the boundaries of others. By recognizing the importance of setting boundaries and practicing these skills, individuals can contribute to healthier and a more fulfilling relationships, personally and professionally, while effectively resolving conflicts when they arise.

CHAPTER VI

Building Empathy and Understanding

Empathy exercises and practices

Empathy is a powerful tool for building understanding and connection in our interactions with others, particularly when dealing with challenging personalities. Challenging individuals may exhibit behaviors that test our patience and trigger emotional reactions. However, by cultivating empathy through exercises and practices, we can better navigate these encounters and promote more positive and constructive relationships. Empathy exercises and practices allow us to develop a more profound understanding of others' perspectives, emotions, and needs, leading to improved communication, conflict resolution, and overall well-being.

Empathy is the capability to recognize, comprehend, and share the emotions and perspectives of another person. It involves both cognitive empathy, which is the capacity to comprehend another person's emotions and thoughts, and emotional empathy, which is the capacity to share in and resonate with another person's feelings. Empathy is a skill that can be established and strengthened through deliberate exercises and practices.

One of the fundamental empathy exercises is active listening. Active listening includes giving your full attention to the speaker, focusing on their words, tone, and body language. It involves suppressing the urge to interrupt or formulate a response while the other person is speaking. Instead, the goal is to truly understand the speaker's perspective and emotions. Active listening fosters empathy by demonstrating a genuine interest in the other person's experience and emotions.

Another valuable empathy exercise involves perspective-taking. Perspective-taking requires you to put yourself in the other person's shoes and try to see the situation from their viewpoint. This exercise helps you understand their motivations, fears, and concerns. It can be specifically valuable when dealing with challenging personalities, as it enables you to appreciate the factors that may be driving their behavior. By acknowledging the validity of their perspective, you can build a foundation for empathy.

Furthermore, empathy can be enhanced through mindfulness practices. Mindfulness involves paying deliberate, non-judgmental attention to the present moment. By practicing mindfulness, you can establish greater self-awareness and emotional regulation, which are crucial components of empathy. When you are more attuned to your own emotions and reactions, you become better equipped to understand and empathize with the emotions of others, even when dealing with challenging personalities.

Journaling is another effective empathy exercise. Keeping a journal permits you to reflect on your interactions with challenging individuals. Write about your thoughts, feelings, and reactions during these encounters. Explore what triggered your emotions and consider the possible underlying reasons for the other person's behavior. Journaling helps you gain insights into your own emotional responses and provides an opportunity to practice empathy by exploring alternative perspectives.

Empathy exercises can also involve role-playing. In a secure and controlled environment, engage in role-play scenarios where you take on the role of the challenging personality and a partner assumes your usual role. This exercise allows you to experience the situation from the other person's perspective and gain a deeper understanding of their challenges and emotions. Role-playing fosters empathy by immersing you in the other person's world.

Another powerful empathy practice is meditation. Loving-kindness meditation, in particular, focuses on cultivating feelings of compassion as well as empathy towards oneself and others. During this meditation, you intentionally send wishes of well-being, happiness, and empathy to different people, including those you may find challenging. Regular meditation can increase your capacity for empathy and promote a more compassionate outlook on challenging personalities.

Empathy is a skill that can significantly improve our interactions with challenging personalities. When we approach these individuals with empathy, we create an environment where understanding and communication can flourish, ultimately leading to more positive outcomes and reduced conflict. Empathy exercises and practices allow us to develop and strengthen this essential skill, fostering deeper connections and promoting emotional well-being.

Moreover, empathy is not only about understanding the emotions and perspectives of others but also about expressing empathy through words and actions. Empathetic responses involve validating the other person's feelings and demonstrating that you care about their well-being. For example, if someone is expressing frustration or distress, an empathetic response might be, "I can see that this situation is really bothering you, and I'm here to support you in any way I can." By acknowledging their emotions and offering support, you convey empathy and create a more supportive and understanding atmosphere.

In addition to empathy exercises and practices, it's necessary to cultivate a mindset of curiosity and open-mindedness when dealing with challenging personalities.

Instead of immediately judging or reacting negatively to their behavior, approach the situation with a sense of curiosity. Ask questions to better comprehend their perspective, and consider the possibility that there may be underlying reasons for their actions. This open-minded approach can lead to more empathetic responses and a deeper understanding of the individual.

Empathy is not always easy, especially when dealing with individuals who exhibit challenging behaviors. It needs patience, practice, and a willingness to suspend judgment. However, the benefits of empathy in building understanding and improving relationships are significant. By incorporating empathy exercises and practices into your daily life and interactions, you can foster a more empathetic mindset and create more harmonious connections with challenging personalities. Ultimately, empathy is a powerful tool for promoting empathy in others and fostering more positive and constructive relationships in all aspects of life.

Practicing forgiveness

Dealing with challenging personalities can be a source of stress, frustration, and conflict in our personal and professional lives. These individuals often exhibit behaviors that test our patience and trigger emotional reactions. However, a powerful approach to fostering empathy and understanding in such situations is the practice of forgiveness. Forgiveness is not only an act of compassion towards others, but it is also a means of healing and growth for ourselves. By exploring the concept of forgiveness and its application in our interactions with challenging personalities, we can create a path towards greater empathy, improved relationships, and emotional well-being.

Forgiveness is a multifaceted concept that involves letting go of negative emotions, resentment, and the desire for revenge or retribution towards someone who has wronged us. It is important to note that forgiveness does not mean condoning or excusing the hurtful behavior of others. Instead, it involves a conscious decision to release the emotional burden associated with the wrongdoing and to move forward with greater empathy and understanding.

One of the key benefits of practicing forgiveness is that it allows us to free ourselves from the emotional weight of resentment and anger. When we hold onto the grudges and negative feelings towards challenging individuals, we carry that emotional baggage with us, impacting our mental and emotional well-being. Forgiveness enables us to release these burdens, providing relief and emotional liberation.

Forgiveness also promotes empathy by encouraging us to see the humanity in others, even when they exhibit challenging behaviors. It invites us to consider the factors that may have contributed to their actions, such as past experiences, insecurities, or struggles. By acknowledging these factors, we can develop a more compassionate perspective, fostering understanding of the individual behind the challenging personality.

Moreover, forgiveness is a means of setting healthy boundaries in our interactions with challenging personalities. It does not require us to tolerate or accept ongoing mistreatment. Instead, forgiveness can be practiced from a distance, allowing us to protect ourselves from harm while still extending empathy and understanding. This approach empowers us to choose the level of engagement we are comfortable with while maintaining emotional well-being.

It is essential to recognize that forgiveness is a process that may take time and effort. It is not always easy, especially when dealing with individuals who have repeatedly hurt or wronged us. However, forgiveness is a journey worth embarking on, as it holds the potential to transform our relationships and emotional state.

Forgiveness begins with a willingness to let go of negative emotions and resentment. This willingness is often rooted in the desire for personal healing and emotional freedom. By acknowledging the emotional toll that holding onto grudges has on our well-being, we can find motivation to start the forgiveness process.

Furthermore, forgiveness involves a process of reframing our perspective on the challenging personality. Instead of focusing solely on their hurtful actions, we can try to comprehend the circumstances and experiences that may have influenced their behavior. This shift in perspective allows us to humanize the individual, recognizing their flaws and vulnerabilities.

Another crucial aspect of forgiveness is setting boundaries to protect ourselves from further harm. Forgiveness does not require us to subject ourselves to ongoing mistreatment. Instead, it allows us to establish healthy boundaries that safeguard our emotional well-being while still extending empathy and understanding.

In addition to individual forgiveness, collective forgiveness can also be significant in healing relationships and promoting empathy. When conflicts arise in group settings, such as families, workplaces, or communities, practicing forgiveness collectively can lead to reconciliation and greater harmony. It involves acknowledging shared responsibility for the conflict, expressing remorse, and working together towards resolution.

Moreover, forgiveness can be a form of self-compassion. By forgiving ourselves for any role we may have played in conflicts or for any negative emotions we may have harbored, we practice self-acceptance and self-compassion. Self-forgiveness is an integral part of the forgiveness process and contributes to our emotional healing and growth.

The practice of forgiveness is not about denying or minimizing the harm caused by challenging personalities. Instead, it is a means of transcending the hurt, anger, and resentment that can perpetuate conflicts and hinder our capacity for empathy and understanding. It allows us to break free from the cycle of negativity and transform our relationships.

Moreover, forgiveness is a continuous practice rather than a single incident. It may require revisiting and reaffirming our forgiveness as new emotions and challenges arise. Forgiveness is a dynamic process that evolves as we grow and change. It is a commitment to emotional well-being and the promotion of empathy in our interactions with challenging personalities.

In conclusion, practicing forgiveness is a powerful means of fostering empathy and understanding when dealing with challenging personalities. It liberates us from the emotional burden of resentment, encourages empathy by humanizing the individual behind the challenging behavior, and allows us to set healthy boundaries to protect our well-being. Forgiveness is a journey of personal healing and growth that can transform our relationships, promote emotional well-being, and contribute to a more compassionate and empathetic world. By embracing forgiveness as a tool for understanding, we open the door to greater empathy, healing, and harmony in our interactions with challenging personalities.

Recognizing common ground

In the realm of human interactions, dealing with challenging personalities can be a daunting task. These individuals often present behaviors, attitudes, and worldviews that are at odds with our own, leading to friction, misunderstandings, and conflicts. However, a powerful strategy for building empathy and understanding in such situations is to recognize common ground. Identifying shared values, goals, and interests provides a foundation for connection and fosters greater empathy, enabling us to navigate interactions with challenging personalities more effectively. By exploring the concept of recognizing common ground and its application in our dealings with difficult individuals, we can pave the way for more harmonious relationships and improved communication.

Recognizing common ground involves finding areas of agreement, shared values, or mutual interests between ourselves and challenging personalities. Even when the differences between two individuals seem insurmountable, there are often underlying commonalities that can serve as a bridge for connection and understanding. This recognition can be a transformative step in fostering empathy and diffusing tension in interactions with challenging individuals.

One of the key benefits of recognizing common ground is that it creates a sense of shared humanity. It reminds us that, despite our differences, we are all human beings with common needs, desires, and emotions. This shared humanity forms the basis for empathy, allowing us to relate to the experiences and feelings of challenging personalities on a fundamental level.

Moreover, recognizing common ground opens the door to constructive dialogue and communication. When we acknowledge shared values or interests, we create a context in which conversations can be more productive and less adversarial. This shift in tone can lead to more open and empathetic interactions, facilitating better understanding and conflict resolution.

In practice, recognizing common ground often begins with active listening. By genuinely listening to the perspectives and viewpoints of challenging personalities, we may uncover areas of agreement or shared values that were previously unnoticed. Active listening involves suspending judgment and genuinely trying to understand the other person's point of view, even if it differs from our own.

Furthermore, asking open-ended questions can be a valuable strategy for discovering common ground. Open-ended questions encourage individuals to share their feelings and thoughts more fully, allowing for a deeper exploration of their values, interests, and motivations. By asking questions that encourage self-expression, we create opportunities for connecting on shared experiences or concerns.

Another essential aspect of recognizing common ground is empathy. Empathy includes not only understanding the emotions and perspectives of others but also expressing understanding and validation. When we convey empathy by acknowledging the validity of someone's feelings or experiences, we create a sense of connection and mutual respect. This expression of empathy can pave the way for more meaningful interactions and understanding with challenging personalities.

Recognizing common ground can also be facilitated through shared experiences or collaborative activities. Engaging in joint projects, volunteering together, or participating in team-building exercises can bring individuals with differing personalities together around a common goal. These shared experiences foster cooperation, trust, and a sense of unity, which can lead to greater empathy and understanding.

Furthermore, recognizing common ground can extend to finding common goals or shared values in a broader context. For instance, in a workplace, colleagues with different personalities may find common ground in their commitment to the organization's mission or their desire to achieve career growth. By aligning their efforts with these shared goals, individuals can work together more effectively and build greater empathy for one another.

In addition to interpersonal interactions, recognizing common ground can be applied to group dynamics and societal issues. In situations where collective decision-making is required, identifying shared values or common goals among diverse stakeholders can lead to more collaborative and empathetic solutions. This approach is particularly relevant in addressing complex societal challenges that require cooperation among individuals, communities, and organizations.

It is important to acknowledge that recognizing common ground does not mean ignoring or minimizing differences. Differences in personality, values, and perspectives will still exist, but by focusing on shared values or interests, we create a foundation for empathy and understanding that can coexist with those differences.

Moreover, recognizing common ground does not require us to compromise our own values or principles. It is possible to find shared values or interests without abandoning our core beliefs. Instead, it involves seeking commonality in areas that do not conflict with our fundamental values.

In conclusion, recognizing common ground is a powerful strategy for building empathy and understanding when dealing with challenging personalities. It reminds us of our shared humanity, opens the door to constructive communication, and fosters greater empathy. By actively listening, asking open-ended questions, expressing empathy, and engaging in shared experiences, we can uncover areas of agreement and connection with challenging individuals. This recognition of common ground can lead to more harmonious relationships, improved communication, and enhanced understanding, ultimately contributing to a more empathetic as well as compassionate world.

Promoting emotional intelligence

Dealing with challenging personalities in our personal and professional lives can be a complex and emotionally taxing experience. These individuals may exhibit behaviors that trigger frustration, anger, or confusion, making it difficult to communicate effectively and foster positive relationships. However, by promoting emotional intelligence, we can significantly enhance our capacity for empathy and understanding when dealing with challenging personalities. Emotional intelligence involves recognizing, understanding, and managing our own emotions while also empathizing with the emotions of others. It provides a foundation for improved communication, conflict resolution, and overall emotional well-being. This section will examine the idea of emotional intelligence and how to use it to your advantage when interacting with difficult people.

A few essential elements of emotional intelligence are self-awareness, self-regulation, empathy, and social skills. Together, these elements improve our capacity to negotiate the complicated terrain of human emotions, including both our own and those of others.

The cornerstone of emotional intelligence is self-awareness. It entails being aware of and cognizant of our own feelings, triggers, and emotional recurring themes. Self-awareness enables us to recognize our emotional responses to challenging personalities' behavior. Developing this awareness is a vital first step in controlling our reactions and avoiding the escalation of emotions. By understanding our emotional triggers, we can choose more constructive ways to react and communicate.

Self-regulation is the ability to manage and control our own emotions effectively. It enables us to remain calm and composed in the face of challenging behavior and to respond thoughtfully rather than reactively. When we encounter challenging personalities, self-regulation helps us avoid escalating conflicts and instead fosters a more empathetic and constructive atmosphere. It allows us to choose our words and actions intentionally, even in emotionally charged situations.

A fundamental component of emotional intelligence is empathy, as it involves understanding and sharing the emotions of others. When dealing with challenging personalities, empathy allows us to see the situation from their perspective and acknowledge their feelings and needs. Empathy humanizes the individual behind the challenging behavior, helping us move beyond judgment and fostering a deeper understanding of their motivations and struggles.

A variety of abilities, including effective communication, active listening, conflict resolution, and teamwork, are included in social skills. These skills are crucial when interacting with challenging personalities. Active listening, for example, allows us to fully understand the other person's perspective and emotions, while effective communication enables us to convey our own thoughts and feelings with clarity and empathy. Conflict resolution and teamwork skills help us navigate challenging interactions and build more positive relationships.

Practicing emotional intelligence when dealing with challenging personalities begins with self-reflection. It involves examining our own emotional reactions and biases, as well as our communication and conflict-resolution skills. By recognizing areas where we can improve our emotional intelligence, we can take proactive steps to enhance our capacity for empathy and understanding.

One practical way to promote emotional intelligence is through mindfulness meditation. Mindfulness entails paying non-judgmental attention to the present moment, including our thoughts, emotions, and bodily sensations. Regular mindfulness practice helps us become more attuned to our own emotions and reactions, allowing us to respond to challenging personalities with greater self-awareness and self-regulation.

In addition to self-awareness, mindfulness meditation fosters empathy by cultivating a more compassionate outlook. When we practice mindfulness, we develop a greater sense of interconnectedness with others and a deeper understanding of the universality of human emotions. This perspective shift promotes empathy and reduces judgment when dealing with challenging individuals.

Another valuable aspect of promoting emotional intelligence is developing active listening skills. Active listening entails offering our full attention to the speaker, focusing on their words, tone, and body language. When interacting with challenging personalities, active listening allows us to fully grasp their perspective and emotions. It also demonstrates our willingness to understand and empathize with their experiences.

Furthermore, effective communication is a key component of emotional intelligence. Clear and empathetic communication involves expressing our thoughts and feelings honestly and respectfully while also actively listening to the other person's viewpoint. When dealing with challenging personalities, effective communication can facilitate more productive and empathetic interactions. It helps convey our understanding and willingness to engage in constructive dialogue.

Conflict resolution skills are also vital in promoting emotional intelligence when dealing with challenging personalities. Conflict is a natural part of human interactions, and it often arises when individuals have differing perspectives or needs. Effective conflict resolution involves finding mutually satisfactory solutions while maintaining empathy and respect. It enables us to address conflicts with challenging individuals in a way that promotes understanding and resolution rather than escalating tensions.

In addition to conflict resolution, teamwork skills are relevant when navigating interactions with challenging personalities, especially in group or professional settings. Teamwork skills include collaboration, cooperation, and the ability to work effectively with diverse individuals. These skills promote a sense of unity and shared goals, fostering empathy and understanding among team members, even when dealing with challenging colleagues. Moreover, empathy exercises and practices can play a significant role in promoting emotional intelligence. These exercises involve consciously seeking to understand the emotions and perspectives of others, including challenging personalities. They can include role-playing, perspective-taking, and journaling about our interactions with these individuals. By actively practicing empathy, we enhance our capacity to relate to the emotions and experiences of others, even in challenging situations.

Promoting emotional intelligence is not about suppressing our own emotions or condoning challenging behavior. It is about recognizing our emotional reactions, managing them efficiently, and empathizing with the emotions of others. It's a skill that can greatly improve our relationships and facilitate conflict resolution when dealing with difficult personalities.

In conclusion, promoting emotional intelligence is a powerful means of building empathy and understanding when dealing with challenging personalities. It involves self-awareness, self-regulation, empathy, and social skills, all of which enhance our capacity to navigate complex emotional interactions. By practicing mindfulness, developing active listening and effective communication skills, and cultivating empathy through exercises and practices, we can approach challenging personalities with greater empathy and understanding. This not only leads to more harmonious relationships but also contributes to our overall emotional well-being and personal growth.

CHAPTER VII

Case Studies and Real-Life Examples

Real-life scenarios illustrating challenges with difficult personalities

In the tapestry of our daily lives, interactions with a diverse array of personalities are inevitable. While many of these encounters are pleasant and productive, there are instances when we find ourselves grappling with individuals who exhibit challenging or difficult personalities. These situations can be emotionally taxing and test our patience, empathy, and conflict resolution skills. Real-life scenarios offer poignant examples of the challenges posed by difficult personalities and provide valuable insights into how we can navigate such encounters with grace and effectiveness.

Scenario 1: The Overbearing Supervisor

Imagine working in a high-pressure corporate environment where your direct supervisor possesses an overbearing and domineering personality. This supervisor frequently micromanages your work, dismisses your input, and often communicates in a condescending manner. The scenario becomes even more challenging when your ideas and efforts are consistently undervalued, leading to frustration and a sense of powerlessness.

In this scenario, it can be particularly difficult to maintain a sense of professionalism and emotional composure. However, effective strategies for dealing with an overbearing supervisor involve a combination of self-regulation and assertiveness. It is essential to manage your emotions, avoid reacting defensively, and maintain open lines of communication. Addressing concerns calmly and constructively while seeking opportunities to demonstrate your value and expertise can lead to improved interactions and potentially reshape the supervisor's behavior over time.

Scenario 2: The Passive-Aggressive Co-worker

In an office setting, you may encounter a co-worker who exhibits passive-aggressive behavior. This individual is skilled at masking their true feelings, often using sarcasm, subtle criticism, or backhanded compliments. The passive-aggressive co-worker tends to avoid direct confrontation while creating an atmosphere of tension and discomfort within the team.

Dealing with passive-aggressive behavior can be challenging, as it can erode trust and undermine effective teamwork. In such scenarios, assertiveness and open communication are essential. Address the behavior directly, expressing your concerns calmly and assertively. Encourage open dialogue and seek to understand the co-worker's perspective. Often, passive-aggressive behavior stems from underlying issues or unexpressed grievances. Creating a safe space for discussion can lead to a more empathetic understanding of the co-worker's concerns and pave the way for conflict resolution.

Scenario 3: The Argumentative Family Member Within

the context of family dynamics, you may encounter a family member known for their argumentative and confrontational personality. Whether it's at holiday gatherings or during everyday conversations, this individual seems to relish engaging in heated debates and rarely backs down from a challenge. The scenario becomes particularly challenging when their confrontational style disrupts family harmony and creates tension.

Dealing with an argumentative family member requires a delicate balance of empathy and boundary-setting. It can be tempting to avoid or appease the confrontations, but this approach may perpetuate the behavior. Instead, assertive communication and setting clear boundaries are key. Express your desire for peaceful and respectful interactions, and calmly disengage from confrontations that escalate. Over time, consistently upholding these boundaries can encourage more considerate behavior from the family member.

Scenario 4: The Inflexible Collaborator

In a professional context, collaborative projects often involve diverse teams with varying personalities. Imagine working on a crucial project with a colleague known for their rigid and inflexible approach. This individual resists compromise, dismisses alternative ideas, and insists on their way of doing things. This rigidity hinders progress and creates frustration among team members.

Navigating collaborations with inflexible individuals calls for a combination of diplomacy and assertiveness. It is important to acknowledge the value of their contributions while also advocating for a more flexible and open-minded approach. Encourage constructive dialogue and present evidence supporting alternative solutions. Building a case based on data and shared goals can often persuade inflexible collaborators to reconsider their positions, fostering a more cooperative and productive atmosphere.

Scenario 5: The Chronic Complainer

Chronic complainers are individuals who habitually focus on the negative aspects of situations and frequently express dissatisfaction or grievances. In both personal and professional settings, dealing with someone who constantly complains can be draining and challenging to manage. Their negativity can permeate the environment and impact morale.

When confronted with a chronic complainer, it is important to maintain empathy while also setting boundaries. Acknowledge their feelings and concerns, but gently redirect the conversation toward constructive solutions or positive aspects when appropriate. Encourage them to participate in problem-solving rather than dwelling solely on the issues. Establishing limits on the time and attention given to complaints can help maintain a more positive and productive atmosphere.

In conclusion, real-life scenarios involving difficult personalities highlight the complexity and emotional challenges that can arise in our interactions with others. These situations serve as powerful reminders of the importance of emotional intelligence, assertiveness, empathy, and effective communication in navigating such encounters. While it may not always be possible to change the behavior of challenging individuals, we can enhance our own skills and responses to foster more positive and productive interactions, ultimately contributing to improved relationships and a more harmonious environment.

How the principles discussed earlier can be applied in these cases

The principles discussed earlier for dealing with challenging personalities offer valuable guidance in navigating real-life scenarios that test our patience, empathy, and conflict resolution skills. Applying these principles can transform difficult interactions into opportunities for growth, understanding, and improved relationships. Let's delve into how these principles can be effectively applied in the cases of challenging personalities outlined in the previous section.

1. The   Overbearing   Supervisor: Self-Regulation   and
Assertiveness

When confronted with an overbearing supervisor, the
principles of self-regulation and assertiveness come into
play. Self-regulation involves managing our own emotions
effectively. In this scenario, it means maintaining
composure and avoiding emotional reactions when the
supervisor's behavior becomes frustrating. Instead of
reacting defensively or resentfully, practice self-
awareness to recognize your emotional triggers and take
a step back before responding.

Assertiveness is crucial for addressing the situation
constructively. It entails expressing your thoughts and
feelings openly and respectfully. Engage in open
communication with your supervisor, calmly and
assertively expressing your concerns about
micromanagement or condescending communication. Use
"I" statements to convey how their behavior affects you
personally, such as "I feel more empowered when I have
the opportunity to take ownership of my tasks."

Furthermore, demonstrate your value and expertise by
seeking opportunities to showcase your skills and
contribute meaningfully to projects. Prove your
competence and professionalism, which may gradually
influence the supervisor's behavior and perceptions. By
combining self-regulation with assertiveness, you can
promote more respectful and productive interactions.

2. The Passive-Aggressive Co-worker: Open
Communication and Conflict Resolution

Dealing with passive-aggressive behavior in a co-worker
requires open communication and conflict resolution
skills. Begin by addressing the behavior directly but
tactfully. Approach the co-worker and express your
concerns in a non-confrontational manner, focusing on the
impact of their actions on the team or work environment.

Use active listening skills to comprehend their perspective, as passive-aggressive behavior often stems from unexpressed grievances or frustrations. Create a safe space for them to voice their concerns and feelings. By listening empathetically, you can uncover the root causes of their behavior and identify potential solutions.

Conflict resolution skills come into play when working towards a resolution. Seek mutually satisfactory solutions and propose compromises that address both parties' needs and concerns. Encourage open dialogue and teamwork to build a more positive and collaborative atmosphere. Consistently upholding these principles can lead to a more empathetic understanding of the co-worker's perspective and a reduction in passive-aggressive behavior.

3. The Argumentative Family Member: Empathy and Boundaries

Interacting with an argumentative family member requires a balance of empathy and setting clear boundaries. Start by empathizing with their need for engagement and their perspectives. Understand that their confrontational behavior may stem from a desire for intellectual stimulation or the need to express themselves.

Express your desire for peaceful and respectful interactions within the family. Emphasize the importance of maintaining harmony and enjoying each other's company during family gatherings. Encourage empathetic listening within the family, where each member takes turns sharing their thoughts and feelings without judgment.

However, it's also crucial to set boundaries. When the family member becomes argumentative or confrontational, calmly disengage from the conversation rather than escalating the conflict. Let them know that you prefer not to engage in arguments and suggest discussing topics that promote harmony. By consistently upholding these boundaries, you can encourage more considerate behavior from the family member while fostering understanding within the family.

4. The Inflexible Collaborator: Diplomacy and Constructive Advocacy

Collaborating with an inflexible individual calls for diplomacy and constructive advocacy. Diplomacy involves maintaining a respectful and tactful approach, even when faced with rigidity. Understand that their inflexibility may be rooted in their strong convictions or the belief that their approach is the most effective.

Advocate for your ideas and alternative solutions using evidence and data to support your case. Emphasize shared goals and the potential benefits of considering different approaches. Encourage constructive dialogue and brainstorming sessions that involve the entire team, fostering a more inclusive decision-making process.

When advocating for flexibility, ensure that your tone is non-confrontational and that you avoid making the individual feel defensive. By focusing on shared objectives and presenting well-reasoned arguments, you can influence the collaborator to consider alternative approaches, ultimately leading to more cooperative and productive teamwork.

5. The Chronic Complainer: Empathy and Redirecting Conversations

Interacting with a chronic complainer requires empathy and the skill to redirect conversations toward solutions or positivity. Begin by acknowledging their feelings and concerns, showing that you comprehend and empathize with their perspective. Validating their emotions can create a more empathetic atmosphere.

However, it's important to gently redirect the conversation when complaints become overwhelming. Encourage the individual to participate in problem-solving or focus on positive aspects of the situation. For example, you can say, "I understand your concerns, but what do you think we can do to address this issue?" or "I appreciate your feedback; let's also discuss what's going well in this situation."

Setting limits on the time and attention given to complaints is another crucial step. Politely express your willingness to listen but indicate that you also want to discuss solutions or positive aspects. By consistently redirecting conversations and maintaining empathy, you can promote a more positive and constructive atmosphere.

In conclusion, the principles discussed for dealing with challenging personalities can be effectively applied in real-life scenarios to transform difficult interactions into opportunities for growth and understanding. Whether it's an overbearing supervisor, a passive-aggressive co-worker, an argumentative family member, an inflexible collaborator, or a chronic complainer, practicing self-regulation, assertiveness, open communication, empathy, conflict resolution, diplomacy, and constructive advocacy can lead to more positive and productive relationships. These principles empower individuals to navigate challenging personalities with grace and effectiveness, ultimately contributing to improved interactions and a more harmonious environment.

CHAPTER VIII

Self-Care and Boundaries

The importance of self-care when dealing with challenging personalities

Navigating interactions with challenging personalities can be emotionally and mentally taxing. Whether it's dealing with an overbearing boss, a passive-aggressive colleague, or an argumentative family member, these encounters can leave you feeling drained and stressed. In such situations, the importance of self-care cannot be overstated. Self-care encompasses a range of practices and strategies aimed at nurturing your well-being and maintaining your mental and emotional health. When dealing with challenging personalities, prioritizing self- care is not a luxury but a necessity. In this essay, we will explore why self-care is essential in these situations and how it can help you cope with the demands of challenging interactions.

First and foremost, self-care acts as a protective shield for your mental and emotional health. Interacting with challenging personalities can trigger a range of negative emotions, including frustration, anger, anxiety, and even self-doubt. These emotions, if left unaddressed, can accumulate and take a toll on your well-being, potentially leading to burnout or emotional exhaustion. Engaging in self-care practices helps you manage and release these emotions, preventing them from overwhelming you.

One crucial component of self-care is setting boundaries. When dealing with challenging personalities, it's essential to establish clear limits on the time and emotional energy you're willing to invest. Boundaries protect you from becoming overly involved or emotionally entangled in difficult interactions. They empower you to step back when necessary, regroup, and recharge.

Furthermore, self-care encompasses stress reduction techniques that can be especially valuable when facing challenging personalities. Activities such as meditation, deep breathing exercises, or physical activity can help minimize stress and anxiety, enabling you to approach interactions with greater calm and composure. By incorporating stress reduction practices into your daily routine, you can better manage the emotional impact of challenging personalities.

Self-care also involves seeking support from your social network. Discussing your experiences and feelings with friends, family members, or a trusted colleague can provide emotional validation and perspective. They can offer valuable insights or simply lend a sympathetic ear, helping you process your emotions and gain clarity on how to navigate difficult situations.

In addition to external support, self-care encourages self-reflection and self-awareness. Take time to assess your own emotional triggers and reactions when dealing with challenging personalities. Self-awareness allows you to recognize when you're becoming emotionally entangled or overwhelmed and prompts you to implement self-care strategies. It also enables you to identify patterns in your responses and explore healthier ways of managing your emotions.

Another essential aspect of self-care is practicing self-compassion. When facing challenging personalities, it's easy to become self-critical, questioning your ability to handle the situation or blaming yourself for the interactions. Self-compassion entails treating yourself with similar kindness and understanding that you would provide to a friend in a similar situation. Remind yourself that dealing with difficult individuals is a challenging endeavor, and it's okay to seek self-care and support.

Additionally, self-care encourages you to engage in activities that bring joy as well as fulfillment into your life. Pursuing hobbies, interests, or creative outlets provides a welcome respite from the stresses of challenging interactions. These activities allow you to recharge, boost your mood, and maintain a sense of balance and well-being.

It's important to determine that self-care is not a one-size-fits-all concept. What constitutes self-care is highly individual and varies from person to person. Some may find solace in spending time in nature, while others may derive comfort from reading, painting, or engaging in physical exercise. The key is to identify activities and practices that resonate with you personally and apply them into your routine.

The benefits of self-care extend beyond immediate relief from the emotional strain of dealing with challenging personalities. Over time, self-care builds resilience, helping you develop the emotional strength to handle difficult interactions more effectively. It equips you with a toolbox of strategies for maintaining your well-being and coping with stressors as they arise.

Furthermore, practicing self-care promotes a positive cycle of self-improvement and personal growth. As you prioritize your mental and emotional health, you become better equipped to respond constructively to challenging personalities. You develop a greater capacity for empathy, assertiveness, and emotional intelligence, which can result in a more harmonious interactions.

In summary, the importance of self-care when dealing with challenging personalities cannot be overstated. It serves as a protective shield for your mental and emotional health, allowing you to manage negative emotions, set boundaries, reduce stress, and seek support. Self-care fosters self-awareness, self- compassion, and personal growth, ultimately empowering you to navigate challenging interactions with grace and resilience. By prioritizing self-care, you not only protect your well-being but also enhance your ability to respond effectively to the demands of challenging personalities, fostering more positive and constructive relationships.

Setting and maintaining healthy boundaries

Dealing with challenging personalities can be a demanding task, one that requires finesse and a firm understanding of the significance of setting and maintaining healthy boundaries. Whether it's a difficult coworker, a family member, or a friend, navigating relationships with individuals who possess challenging personalities can be emotionally taxing and mentally draining. However, establishing and upholding boundaries is essential for preserving your well-being and ensuring that these relationships do not become detrimental to your mental health.

First and foremost, it's crucial to recognize the significance of boundaries in any relationship. Boundaries are known as the invisible lines which define the limits of acceptable behavior, communication, and interaction within a relationship. When dealing with challenging personalities, setting these boundaries becomes even more crucial, as these individuals often push the limits and may not respect personal space or emotional boundaries naturally. Without clear boundaries, you risk becoming entangled in their drama, manipulation, or negativity, which can lead to emotional turmoil and stress.

Setting healthy boundaries begins with self-awareness. You must understand your own needs, values, and limits before you can effectively communicate them to others. Reflect on what is important to you, what makes you uncomfortable, and where you draw the line. Once you have a clear understanding of your own boundaries, you can start communicating them assertively but respectfully. This may involve expressing your feelings, needs, and limits directly and honestly to the challenging individual. Keep in mind that setting boundaries is not a sign of weakness but a sign of self-respect and self-care.

When setting boundaries with challenging personalities, it's crucial to remain consistent and firm in your communication. Challenging individuals may test your boundaries repeatedly, hoping to wear you down and gain the upper hand. Therefore, you must maintain your stance and not give in to manipulation or emotional pressure. Be prepared for resistance or pushback, but stay resolute in your commitment to your own well-being. Setting boundaries can also be greatly aided by nonverbal cues in addition to verbal communication. You can communicate your feelings and boundaries to the difficult person through your body language, tone of voice, and facial expressions. You can effectively reinforce your boundaries by keeping eye contact, sitting or standing at a comfortable distance, and using a firm but respectful tone of voice.

One of the challenges in dealing with challenging personalities is the potential for guilt or fear of confrontation. You may worry about hurting their feelings or damaging the relationship. However, it's essential to remember that setting boundaries is not about hurting others but about protecting yourself. Healthy boundaries can lead to healthier relationships in the long run, as they create a foundation of mutual respect and understanding. Another crucial aspect of boundary-setting is recognizing when it's time to distance yourself from toxic individuals. In some cases, despite your best efforts, certain people may consistently violate your boundaries, show no willingness to change, or have a detrimental impact on your mental health. In such situations, it may be necessary to limit or even sever ties with these individuals for your own well-being. While this can be a difficult decision, it is sometimes the only way to protect yourself from ongoing harm.

Maintaining healthy boundaries is an ongoing process. It requires self-awareness, assertiveness, and a commitment to self-care. It also involves regular self-assessment to ensure that your boundaries continue to align with your evolving needs and values. As you grow and change, your boundaries may need adjustment to accommodate new circumstances and relationships.

In conclusion, setting and maintaining healthy boundaries when dealing with challenging personalities is essential for preserving your mental and emotional well-being. Recognize the importance of boundaries, understand your own limits, communicate assertively, and be prepared to stand firm in the face of resistance. Remember that setting boundaries is an act of self-respect and self-care, and it can lead to healthier and a more fulfilling relationships in the long run.

Avoiding burnout and compassion fatigue

Dealing with challenging personalities in our personal and professional lives can be emotionally and mentally taxing. Whether it's a demanding boss, a difficult coworker, or a family member with complex issues, the stress and frustration that can arise from such interactions can lead to burnout and compassion fatigue if not managed effectively. This section explores the strategies and practices that can help individuals avoid burnout and compassion fatigue while dealing with challenging personalities.

Burnout is a state of emotional, mental, as well as physical exhaustion resulting from prolonged stress and overwork. It often occurs when individuals consistently face challenging situations without adequate coping mechanisms or support. When dealing with challenging personalities, it's important to know the signs of burnout, which may include feelings of chronic fatigue, cynicism, reduced effectiveness, and detachment from one's responsibilities or relationships. To prevent burnout, it's crucial to prioritize self-care. This includes setting boundaries, practicing stress management techniques, and taking regular breaks to recharge.

Compassion fatigue, on the other hand, is a unique form of burnout that specifically affects individuals in caregiving or helping professions, such as healthcare workers, therapists, and social workers. However, it can also impact anyone who regularly interacts with challenging personalities. Compassion fatigue arises from the emotional toll of empathizing with others' suffering and stress. When dealing with challenging personalities, it's common to experience compassion fatigue because these individuals often have their own emotional struggles. To avoid compassion fatigue, it's important to establish healthy emotional boundaries. While empathy and compassion are valuable, they should not come at the expense of your own well-being. To lessen compassion fatigue, engage in self-compassion practices and seek out support from friends, family, or a therapist.

One effective strategy for avoiding burnout and compassion fatigue when dealing with challenging personalities is self-awareness. It's essential to recognize your own limits and vulnerabilities. Understand the specific triggers that lead to stress and frustration in your interactions with challenging individuals. By acknowledging these triggers, you can develop proactive strategies to manage them. Self-awareness also involves regularly checking in with your own emotional state and seeking support or professional help when needed.

Another crucial aspect of avoiding burnout and compassion fatigue is setting and maintaining healthy boundaries. Challenging personalities often push boundaries and may not respect personal space or emotional limits naturally. Therefore, it's essential to establish clear boundaries and communicate them assertively but respectfully. This may involve saying no when necessary, limiting the time spent with challenging individuals, or setting limits on the emotional energy you invest in these relationships. Boundaries serve as a protective shield against the emotional toll of dealing with difficult people.

In addition to setting boundaries, practicing self-care is paramount. Self-care encompasses activities and habits that nourish your physical, emotional, and mental well-being. It can include exercise, meditation, hobbies, spending time with loved ones, or simply taking time for yourself. Consistently prioritizing self-care helps build resilience and prevents the accumulation of stress as well as exhaustion that can lead to burnout as well as compassion fatigue.

Seeking support is another valuable strategy. Sharing your experiences and challenges with trusted friends, family members, or colleagues can provide emotional validation and a sense of community. Moreover, professional support from a therapist or a counselor can offer guidance and coping strategies tailored to your specific situation.

Finally, it's important to remember that dealing with challenging personalities is not solely your responsibility. Sometimes, individuals with challenging personalities may need professional help or intervention beyond what you can provide. Recognize when it's appropriate to involve others, such as HR professionals, supervisors, or mental health professionals, in managing these challenging interactions.

In conclusion, avoiding burnout and compassion fatigue when dealing with challenging personalities requires self-awareness, boundary setting, self-care, seeking support, and recognizing when additional help is needed. By implementing these strategies, individuals can protect their well-being and maintain their resilience in the face of challenging relationships and interactions. Keep in mind that self-care is not selfish; it is essential for your own health and effectiveness in dealing with life's challenges.

CHAPTER IX

The Path to Lasting Harmony

The journey towards lasting harmony with difficult personalities

Interacting with difficult personalities is an inevitable aspect of life. Whether it's a contentious coworker, an obstinate family member, or a friend with challenging traits, navigating these relationships can be a demanding and often frustrating journey. However, it's essential to recognize that achieving lasting harmony with difficult personalities is not an unattainable goal. With patience, understanding, and effective communication, it is possible to build and maintain healthier, more harmonious relationships.

The first step on the journey towards lasting harmony with difficult personalities is self-reflection. It's essential to examine your own reactions and emotions when dealing with such individuals. Self-awareness allows you to identify your triggers and emotional responses, helping you gain control over your reactions. By understanding your own role in the relationship dynamic, you can work towards managing your emotions more effectively, which in turn can positively impact the interaction with the challenging individual.

Empathy is a critical element in fostering harmony with difficult personalities. While it may be challenging to empathize with someone who consistently exhibits challenging behaviors, it's important to remember that everyone has their struggles and experiences. Attempting to understand their perspective, motivations, and emotions can lead to more compassionate and effective interactions. Empathy can also reduce defensiveness and open the door to productive communication.

Communication is the cornerstone of building lasting harmony with difficult personalities. Effective communication involves active listening, expressing your thoughts and feelings assertively but respectfully, and seeking common ground. It's crucial to create an open and non-judgmental space where both parties feel heard and valued. Avoiding blame and criticism and focusing on finding solutions together can lead to more constructive conversations.

Setting boundaries is another essential component of achieving harmony with difficult personalities. Boundaries assist in defining the limits of acceptable behavior and communication in the relationship. Clear and assertive boundary-setting is necessary to protect your own well-being and prevent manipulation or emotional drain. It's essential to communicate your boundaries clearly and consistently, reinforcing them as needed.

Patience is a virtue when dealing with difficult personalities. Change does not happen overnight, and some individuals may resist altering their behavior or attitudes. Recognize that progress may be slow and intermittent. Be prepared for setbacks, but maintain your commitment to building a more harmonious relationship. Consistency in your own actions and responses can, over time, influence the behavior of the challenging individual.

Sometimes, seeking external support or professional help can be a beneficial part of the journey towards lasting harmony. Mediators, therapists, or counselors can provide guidance, strategies, and a neutral perspective that can facilitate productive conversations and conflict resolution. In some cases, involving a trusted third party can help break down communication barriers and lead to breakthroughs in understanding.

Forgiveness is a potent tool on the path to lasting harmony with difficult personalities. Holding onto grudges or past conflicts can hinder progress and perpetuate negativity. Forgiveness is releasing yourself from the weight of anger and resentment, refraining from approving or justifying harmful behavior. It can open the door to a fresh start and the potential for improved interactions.

Lastly, remember that you have control over your own reactions and choices. While you may not be able to change the challenging individual, you can choose how you respond to their behavior. Cultivate resilience and a positive mindset, focusing on your own growth and well-being. This empowerment can contribute to lasting harmony by reducing the emotional toll of dealing with difficult personalities.

In conclusion, achieving lasting harmony with difficult personalities is a journey that requires self-reflection, empathy, effective communication, boundary-setting, patience, external support when needed, forgiveness, and personal empowerment. While it may be challenging, the rewards of healthier, more harmonious relationships are well worth the effort. By taking proactive steps and approaching the relationship with an open heart and mind, you can transform difficult interactions into opportunities for growth and connection.

Celebrating progress and small victories

Interacting with difficult personalities can be a challenging and sometimes frustrating experience. Whether it's a coworker with a confrontational attitude, a family member with stubborn tendencies, or a friend with an overbearing nature, these relationships can test your patience and resilience. However, it's important to recognize that even in the midst of difficulties, there are opportunities for growth and positive change. One effective approach to improving these relationships is by celebrating progress and small victories along the way.

First and foremost, it's crucial to acknowledge that lasting change in any relationship takes time. Difficult personalities often have ingrained habits and behaviors that are not easily altered. However, by recognizing and appreciating even the smallest steps towards improvement, you can encourage and reinforce positive changes. This not only benefits the challenging individual but also contributes to a more harmonious and satisfying relationship for both parties.

One way to celebrate progress is through positive reinforcement. When the difficult personality exhibits behavior that aligns with your desired outcomes, provide positive feedback and acknowledgment. This can be as easy as offering a genuine compliment, expressing gratitude, or showing appreciation for their efforts. Positive reinforcement encourages the individual to continue moving in the right direction.

Another effective strategy is setting achievable goals. Collaborate with the challenging personality to establish specific, realistic objectives for the relationship. These goals should be small and manageable, focusing on incremental changes rather than dramatic shifts. When these goals are reached, celebrate them together as a shared accomplishment. This creates a sense of partnership and mutual success.

Small victories can also be found in improved communication. When the difficult personality shows a willingness to listen, communicate openly, or engage in constructive dialogue, take notice and appreciate these moments. Effective communication is often a significant challenge in such relationships, so any progress in this area should be acknowledged and celebrated.

In some cases, boundary-setting can be a significant milestone. When the difficult personality respects your boundaries, whether they relate to personal space, time constraints, or emotional limits, it's a sign of progress. Celebrate these instances as indications of improved understanding and respect in the relationship.

Moreover, recognize that setbacks are a natural part of any journey towards better interactions with difficult personalities. It's important not to become discouraged by occasional regressions in behavior or attitudes. Instead, view setbacks as opportunities for learning and growth. Emphasize the importance of resilience and the commitment to progress, even when faced with challenges.

The celebration of progress is not only about acknowledging the changes in the challenging personality but also about nurturing your own well-being. These celebrations can serve as reminders of the positive aspects of the relationship and provide motivation to continue working towards improvement. They can also help you maintain a more optimistic outlook, reducing stress and frustration.

While celebrating progress and small victories is valuable, it's essential to manage your expectations realistically. Not all difficult personalities will undergo significant transformations, and some may never fully change. The goal is not necessarily complete transformation but rather the creation of a more functional and harmonious dynamic.

In conclusion, celebrating progress and small victories with difficult personalities can be a powerful tool for improving these challenging relationships. By acknowledging and appreciating even the smallest steps towards positive change, you create a positive and encouraging environment for both parties. This approach promotes mutual growth, improved communication, and a more satisfying relationship overall. Remember that while change may be slow, the journey towards better interactions is a worthwhile endeavor that can lead to greater understanding and harmony with difficult personalities.

The rewards of finding common ground

Dealing with challenging personalities can be a difficult endeavor, often requiring patience, empathy, and effective communication. However, amidst the initial frustrations and conflicts, there are significant rewards to be gained from finding common ground and building better relationships with such individuals. This essay explores the numerous benefits and personal growth opportunities that arise from the pursuit of common ground with difficult personalities.

One of the most compelling rewards of finding common ground with difficult personalities is the potential for personal growth and development. Navigating these challenging relationships forces individuals to enhance their emotional intelligence, communication skills, as well as conflict resolution abilities. It encourages self-reflection and self-awareness as you learn to manage your emotions and reactions in the face of adversity. Over time, these skills can extend beyond the specific relationship, benefiting your interactions with others and enhancing your overall emotional intelligence.

Building common ground with difficult personalities often leads to improved communication. As you work to understand their perspective and motivations, you may find that the lines of communication open up, allowing for more productive and meaningful conversations. This improved communication can lead to greater clarity and mutual understanding, reducing misunderstandings and conflicts. It fosters an environment where both parties feel heard and respected, paving the way for more harmonious interactions.

Empathy is a vital component of finding common ground, and it goes hand in hand with understanding. Attempting to see the world through the eyes of the challenging personality can lead to increased empathy, which benefits not only the relationship but also your overall ability to relate to others. Empathy enables you to connect on a more profound level and establish a sense of shared humanity, bridging the gap between differences and facilitating genuine connection.

Finding common ground also offers the opportunity to promote positive change in the challenging individual. By demonstrating understanding and respect, you can influence their behavior and attitudes in a more constructive direction. Recognizing their efforts and acknowledging their positive actions can be a powerful motivator for continued growth and personal development. In this way, you become a catalyst for positive change, contributing to their overall well-being.

Moreover, fostering common ground with difficult personalities can lead to a more peaceful as well as harmonious environment. Whether it's at work, within your family, or in your social circle, reduced tension and conflict can create a sense of calm as well as stability. This improved atmosphere benefits not only the individuals directly involved but also those in their proximity, leading to a more positive and enjoyable overall experience.

In some cases, building common ground can transform a challenging relationship into a valuable and supportive one. As you work through conflicts and misunderstandings, you may discover shared interests, goals, or values that were previously overshadowed by the difficulties. These commonalities can form the foundation of a stronger and more meaningful connection, turning a challenging relationship into a source of mutual support and camaraderie.

Lastly, finding common ground with difficult personalities can bring a profound sense of satisfaction and personal fulfillment. Overcoming the obstacles and conflicts that once plagued the relationship can be immensely rewarding. It reinforces your resilience and the belief that positive change is possible, even in the face of adversity. It also provides a sense of accomplishment, as you witness the fruits of your efforts in the form of a more harmonious and functional relationship.

In conclusion, while dealing with difficult personalities may initially seem daunting, the rewards of finding common ground are numerous and profound. These rewards encompass personal growth, improved communication, increased empathy, the potential for positive change in the challenging individual, a more peaceful environment, the possibility of transforming the relationship, and a deep sense of satisfaction and fulfillment. By embracing the challenge and seeking common ground, individuals can unlock the hidden potential for growth, connection, and harmony in their relationships with difficult personalities.

CONCLUSION

In the pages of "Harmony in Conflict: Finding Common Ground with Challenging Personalities," we have embarked on a journey of understanding and transformation. Throughout this book, we explored the intricacies of various personality types, delved into the depths of human psychology, and unearthed effective strategies for navigating the complex terrain of challenging interactions.

As we conclude our exploration, it is evident that harmony in conflict is not an unattainable ideal but a skill that can be cultivated and honed. We have learned that by embracing principles of empathy, self-awareness, assertiveness, and active communication, we can bridge the divides that often separate us from those with challenging personalities.

Furthermore, we have underscored the importance of self-care and healthy boundaries as essential tools in our toolkit for maintaining emotional well-being while engaging with difficult individuals. These practices not only shield us from the emotional toll of challenging interactions but also empower us to foster more positive and constructive relationships.

In the pursuit of harmony, it is crucial to remember that our journey is ongoing. We may encounter setbacks, and our skills will continue to evolve. However, armed with the knowledge and techniques presented in this book, we are better equipped to navigate the complex dynamics of challenging personalities with grace, compassion, and resilience.

As we close the final chapter of "Harmony in Conflict," may we carry forward the wisdom and insights gleaned within these pages into our daily lives, fostering greater understanding, empathy, and harmonious relationships with all those we encounter.

Thank you for buying and reading/ listening to our book. If you found this book useful/ helpful please take a few minutes and leave a review on the platform where you purchased our book. Your feedback matters greatly to us.